Jody,
HERE'S YOR

10631421

Speak As Well As You Think

AN EXECUTIVE'S GUIDE
TO EXCELLENCE
IN PUBLIC SPEAKING

JOHN M. VAUTIER

AND

JOHN J. VAUTIER

Published by Nostina
P.O. Box 7074
Novi, Michigan 48376-7074
nostina.com

Copyright © 2013 John M. Vautier and John J. Vautier

All rights reserved. No part of this book may be reproduced or transmitted
in any form or by any means whatsoever without express written permission
from one of the authors, except in the case of brief quotations
embodied in critical articles and reviews.

ISBN: 0-9815105-9-0
ISBN-13: 978-0-9815105-9-0

THIS BOOK IS DEDICATED TO:

My grandfather, **J. A. Ludlow**, who was born on Christmas Eve 1895, and who died on the Fourth of July 1990. Granddad was as close to a father as I had growing up. One of the original "Curb Brokers" on Wall Street, he founded J. A. Ludlow and Company, was one of the Governors of the American Stock Exchange, and also was Mayor of Saltaire, New York, from 1954 to 1962. I learned discipline, hard work, responsibility, humility and charity from Granddad, and his faith in me was constant. He was fond of saying, "If so-and-so can do it, so can you."

Kevin Daley, Charlie Windhorst and **Jim Smith**, who took a risk back in 1985 on hiring a 24-year-old business forms salesman from Chicago and letting him "grow up" in Communispond. I learned everything I know about sales and coaching from Kevin, Charlie and Jim and the team they assembled at the greatest company in the world. And what a team! Everything we touched turned to gold. I was given experiences way beyond my age, and experience, and my maturity. And I owe Vautier Communications and the skills I have and am passing along, to these great people and the great company they founded.

Ed Kelly, my father-in-law and best friend. Ed is the father I never had. He taught me how to love and lead a family, how to cherish my wife, develop and love our kids, and give thanks to God every day on bended knees for this wonderful life we're blessed with. I love him dearly.

And finally, my wife **Kit**. She's my other best friend, as well as my soul mate and life partner. Kit has supported me, raised our three wonderful kids when I was traveling and coaching and learning the skills that would support us. Kit has managed every detail in our family, and—since 2006—in our business. She's been there through the big transitions and through all the small and wonderful miracles. She has made my life complete. Everything in my life that is of value has to do with her.

**No one can achieve the level of success
we have been blessed to experience
without the help of many wonderful people along the way.
Our thanks go out to:**

Kevin Daley, Charlie Windhorst, Gerry Barandes, Jim Smith, Ted Fuller, Nancy Heckel, Mike Leary, Emmett Wolfe, Lee Melchior, Bob Parkinson, Holly Church and all the other spectacular "Communisponders" who made that original company so successful and took me along with them.

Madeline Borkin, one of the greatest sales people and human beings I have ever had the pleasure to work with and know, who said to me, on a cold April day in 2004, over lunch in Chicago, "John, you should do what you're good at! You should start your own company and we'll be your first client." And that indeed is how Vautier Communications started.

Chuck and Mary Ann Bogosta. Friends forever, who invited me into the University of Pittsburgh Medical Center and Pearson Education and opened up two strong organizations which became the companies that supported our growth in the early days and which continue to work with us today.

And finally, Jessica Hatchigan, who has managed, organized, interviewed, edited and coached me through this project we refer to as "The Book." She has amazing talent with a soft and patient touch and has made this project much easier that I ever thought possible.

—John M. Vautier

CONTENTS

FOREWORD

You are holding in your hands a tool for transformation.

If you are a businessperson, you need to know how to present to a group ably and effectively. This book is designed to help you do just that, and do it consistently.

No doubt you have observed that some people present extraordinarily well. They speak to a group of decision makers and clinch a deal, or get the go-ahead on a project.

In the business world, a presentation—one human being speaking to a group—is the engine that drives almost all decisions in which money changes hands, actions are authorized, or power is deployed. So, if there is one skill area a leader who aims to advance in his or her career needs to master, it is communication skills.

This was an observation I made as a 20-something account executive with J. Walter Thompson, then the largest ad agency in the world, back in the 1970's.

It was brought home to me the day I oversaw the presentations five of JWT's best people made to a potential new client, a Fortune 100. It would, of course, have been a coup for us to sign the client. But we didn't get that account. Analyzing why, it was clear to me that it wasn't because the products and services we offered were lacking in any way. In fact, the sample commercials we aired for the client were great. I knew that something else was responsible for the "no sale."

As I thought about it, I realized the problem: The commercials were fine, but the presenters had failed to impress the client. They were capable—in fact, the best we had. But the client had judged—unfairly, I felt—that the caliber of the people running these key pieces of business for the agency was not impressive enough.

I knew the caliber of the JWT presenters. They were the best. But they hadn't been able to impress that upon the client.

This made me think, there's got to be some kind of program that helps seasoned presenters get better. Because, like it or not, the reality is, speeches and presentations determine the fate of deals in the business community. They are the engine for business getting done.

Determined that we not repeat our error, I looked into finding a training program for our seasoned executives. And I discovered there wasn't such a thing. There was the Dale Carnegie course. It was excellent in its own right. I was a fan of Carnegie training. I had undergone it myself and afterward moonlighted as a Carnegie instructor one evening a week for a couple of years. But Carnegie training, at that time, was geared to a general audience and focused on diverse skills, not simply presenting skills. I discovered there was no program geared to enabling top level business people to present their value propositions in the polished manner needed in order to get new business—or to enabling them to obtain big commitments inside a company to invest money in a project.

For the next two years, together with my partner, Charlie Windhorst, I worked at developing just this kind of program. Charlie and I set up a research model through which we collected and analyzed information. With that in place we then started to conduct two-day classes in JWT's New York City office. Our focus was purely and simply on how to make business executives more effective when speaking or presenting.

One fundamental principle guided our thinking in developing our program: "The only way to judge a talk is by its effect on the listener." Listener feedback was essential, and we developed a process to collect it. The first assignment for enrollees in our early programs was to talk about the most interesting project they were working on at the moment. On a flip chart next to them as they spoke, we had two headings. One heading was "what you see," the other was "what you hear." While one speaker presented, the others in the program observed what worked well and what didn't, and provided feedback. We noted the feedback and collected the data. It was all tested, tried, adjusted and honed. First with a hundred participants, then with a thousand.

Using feedback from the groups, we made discoveries that would greatly advance executive presentation skills training. We paid attention to nuances and drilled down on specific skills—how a speaker stood, moved, gestured, and made eye contact, and on the volume, inflection and pacing of his voice.

The name my partner and I gave the resulting new process we developed to train speakers was Communispond, a combination of "communicate" and "respond." The Communispond system was launched in 1972. Nothing like it had ever existed before. And the results were extraordinary. To date, the training has helped thousands of speakers advance their skills.

The intangibles, such as confidence, conviction, commitment, credibility and enthusiasm—how do you get those across? They're concepts. You don't instill those in an audience through logic. But an outstanding speaker sparks these in an audience. You end up buying the speaker because you believe him and you believe in what he's saying. And you believe him because of physical things—the way he looks to you, the way he gestures, the quality of his voice.

The physical aspects of the speaker convey the sense that he is committed or confident or enthusiastic, and this is transmitted to the audience. So, again, the intangibles are communicated physically.

The philosopher Thomas Aquinas once said, "Nothing enters the human mind except through the senses." What this means is that the body teaches the brain; the brain does not teach the body. This is a fundamental principle of the Communispond tradition. Successful speakers and presenters utilize their bodies in specific ways—ways that may not, at first, feel comfortable to a speaker new to the podium or to presenting. But just as a beginning cyclist eventually "gets the hang of it," so too do speakers who acquire a proven effective set of skills in giving a speech or a presentation.

Habits, after all, are not intellectual. They are physical. The body has to know its role, and then it will behave beautifully. But the brain doesn't control it. It can't. The body has to know. For that reason, Communispond is based upon doing—and on knowledge acquired through doing, rather than knowledge gained through learning. Emerson said: "If you can do a thing once, you can do it twice. And if you can do it twice, you can make a habit out of it."

To date, more than 650,000 participants have been through the Communispond process, and gifted coaches like John M. Vautier— who originally was a regional manager for Communispond and one of the company's stars—have launched their own coaching businesses, building on what they have learned in the Communispond system to advance their own training systems.

This book by John and his son, young John, captures the elements of a program which remains the gold standard for executive communications coaching and presents them in a clear and cogent manner. Clients who have trained with the Vautiers will find this a valuable "refresher." Those who have not yet had the opportunity to work with them will find it a valuable aid in upping their game when it comes to public speaking and presenting.

It is my pleasure to highly recommend this book to any business-person seeking to speak or present as ably and effectively as possible.

Kevin Daley
Communispond Founder
Adjunct Professor, Fordham University
Graduate School of Business

1 - What Happens When You Speak As Well As You Think?

- Doors (And Minds) Open When You 'Speak As Well As You Think'
- How One CEO Used Direct Answers to Turn a Media Disaster into a Non-Story
- How a 15-Minute Presentation Secured a Billion-Dollar Deal
- How One Debate Performance *Almost* Turned a Losing Campaign Around
- How a U.S. President Reframed a National Disaster As a Pioneer's Challenge
- How a U.S. Secretary of State Stayed Bulletproof Under Fire
- The Good News: What They've Learned, *You* Can Too

What does it mean to "speak as well as you think"?

It means that when you get up to present, you are described with words like: *credible, confident, interesting, genuine, natural, compelling, organized, professional, passionate, clear, concise,* and *charismatic.*

Why? Because listeners are wired to instantly attribute positive qualities to men and women who are cool, composed and effective at the podium, and in interviews and meetings. The reason for this is that most people—an estimated 75% of us—experience anxiety when we are called upon to speak publicly. So, all other things being equal, we view professionals who speak and present well as (to sum up all the adjectives above) smart, likable and attractive.

> # Speak as well as you think,
>
> # & your messages
>
> # drive your business results.

Decision makers like promoting smart, likable and attractive people; smart, likable and attractive people also tend to attract opportunities. That's why polishing your public speaking skills widens your avenues for career growth.

Doors (& Minds) Open

When You

'Speak As Well As You Think'

SPEAK AS WELL AS YOU THINK, AND YOU CAN:

- *CREATE CHANGE*, by selling your ideas, products or services internally and externally, and by having your recommendations accepted. (You communicate critical internal and external messages in a clear, crisp and compelling manner.)

- *BUILD CREDIBILITY*, by clearly and concisely delivering news, updates and strategies. (You build your stature internally and externally; you become the leader who gets quoted as an expert source.)

- **LEAD OTHERS**, by obtaining "buy in" when you share your organization's vision, goals and results. (People who hear your messages act on them, understand them and believe in them.)

Let's look at some real-world examples.

How One CEO

Used Direct Answers

to Turn a Media Disaster

into a Non-Story

In April 2010, a British Petroleum oil rig exploded in the Gulf of Mexico. It caused the largest accidental marine oil spill in petroleum industry history. It remains one of the worst environmental disasters of recent decades.

In July 2010, TV news interviewer and journalist George Stephanopoulos interviewed Robert Dudley, newly appointed CEO of British Petroleum, and grilled him on the disastrous spill.

Dudley's responses were direct and affirmed the following:
- The scope of what he called BP's "terribly tragic accident."
- The cause for the spill—safety violations initiated a decade prior to the spill.
- BP set aside $32 billion meant to address the ramifications of the spill.
- Ongoing, BP would hold itself to a "higher standard" and would cooperate with newer, more stringent U.S. regulations.
- BP intended to stay on a growth path while dealing with divestments due to the spill.

Dudley answered Stephanopoulos's questions directly, acknowledging BP's responsibility and shortcomings, and stating clearly the company's actions to compensate for the spill, to ensure that another disaster would never occur, and to put BP on a healthy growth track despite its smaller size due to divestments.

The thorough, direct responses answered media and public concerns. BP eventually would be ordered to pay a historically large settlement. But, in the interim, Dudley's forthright responses halted further damage to the company's reputation and brand. In effect, Dudley's approach defused the story.

How a 15-Minute Presentation Secured a Billion-Dollar Deal

As president of the University of Pittsburgh Medical Center's International and Commercial Services Division, executive Chuck Bogosta—a longtime friend who also is a client of Vautier Communications—is responsible for the expansion of his organization's world-class medical care, technology and services to patients and hospitals around the world.

In 2011, Chuck was contacted by officials in Kazakhstan, the largest of the former Soviet republics, and asked to conduct a feasibility study. The study was to focus on how UPMC would approach developing a national oncology treatment and research center in Kazakhstan, where more than 30,000 new cases of cancer are detected annually—with over half of all cancer patients being diagnosed at a late stage.

"I was told to prepare two things," Chuck says. "First, it was important to prepare a detailed backgrounder document. In

Kazakhstan, deals of this size require that you provide, literally, reams of data—enough to make a good solid thunk when the document lands on a desk. So we did that. Second, I also was told to prepare a verbal presentation, which I did—a 25-page PowerPoint."

Then, Chuck says, it was a matter of awaiting a call from Kazakhstan—a go ahead for him to fly there to give his presentation.

"The call came on a Thursday," he says, "requesting that I present my data and recommendations on a Monday.

"I booked a flight to Kazakhstan for Saturday. I was scheduled to attend a friend's wedding that Saturday. I left halfway through the wedding, got to the airport, flew to Philadelphia, then from Philadelphia to London, from London to Vienna, and from there to Astana, the capital of Kazakhstan—a total flight time of about 30 hours. After a quick clean-up at the hotel, a driver chauffeured me to the prime minister's office and I made my presentation. It lasted 15 minutes and I presented in English. No one except the translator spoke English.

"The prime minister thanked me, and I left to wait outside. Fifteen minutes later, I was called back in. The deal had been approved."

Shortly afterwards, the president of Kazakhstan announced a billion-dollar initiative to build the nation's most advanced oncology treatment and research center, in partnership with UPMC. The center will incorporate the tactics used by UPMC to successfully integrate care, research and medical education at UPMC Cancer Center in order to provide care for citizens of Kazakhstan, and of Eurasia.

In effect, Chuck brokered a billion-dollar deal on the strength of that 15-minute presentation.

"We conducted a lot of the preliminary business via Skype," Chuck says. "And that was very helpful. But for the final presentation—at which a decision would be made—it was vital to the officials in Kazakhstan than I be there in person, even if my presentation was only 15 minutes long. For a deal of this magnitude, nothing replaces face-to-face."

That, of course, is why executives need to master the skills of executive presence in delivering speeches and presentations. The hallmarks of executive presence are professionalism, credibility, and the ability to inspire confidence—even when a translator is required to translate your messages.

And that is how billion-dollar deals are made.

How One Debate

Almost Turned Around

a Losing Campaign

If anyone seeks an example of the power of effective public speaking and executive presence, they need only review the aftermath of the first Presidential Debate of 2012.

In 2012, Republican challenger Mitt Romney was losing significant ground in public opinion polls to incumbent President Barack Obama. President Obama was in the lead across the country, and in battleground States. Governor Romney was doing so poorly in the polls that funding from his own party slowed considerably.

But when Governor Romney forcefully debated the President in the first Presidential Debate, the polls reversed dramatically in his favor—and the talk about lack of funding stopped.

It was only when President Obama found his footing and began to spar effectively with Governor Romney in the second and third debates that he regained the significant ground he had lost in the first debate and then went on to win the election.

How a U.S. President Reframed a National Disaster as a Pioneer's Challenge

In 1986, the Space Shuttle Challenger exploded. The disaster killed all seven astronauts on board, including high school science teacher Christa McAuliffe. The nation was stunned. Some critics called for a halt to the space exploration program.

President Ronald Reagan's speech, delivered a few hours following the Challenger explosion, reframed the disaster for a nation in mourning and helped promote its healing. President Reagan honored the fallen astronauts, acknowledged the nation's pain, and transformed the tragedy into a tribute to the pioneering spirit.

Three days later, at the Johnson Space Center, he reiterated the theme of the price pioneers pay for progress: "Sometimes, when we reach for the stars, we fall short. But we must pick ourselves up again and press on despite the pain."

(Search Google.com with the terms "Reagan Challenger disaster speech" to find the text of this speech online; search YouTube.com with the same terms to view the video.)

Peggy Noonan, who wrote the speech, based on input from President Reagan, describes the composition process in her book *What I Saw at the Revolution*. Perhaps the most fascinating observation she makes is that immediately upon finishing the speech, President Reagan felt the speech might not have fully accomplished its mission: to laud those lost in the explosion, and to reassure the nation.

But, Noonan writes, "The next morning there was a deluge"—of positive response. She also notes that an aide tried to tamper with the closing line, to make it echo a commercial he had heard that he felt was "eloquent." Of course, had he done so, it would have marred a speech that is now considered a classic. Peggy Noonan, of course, fought this suggestion ferociously, as would any speechwriter worth her pen and ink—and the rest is history.

We will never forget them, nor the last time we saw them, this morning, as they prepared for the journey and waved goodbye and "slipped the surly bonds of earth" to "touch the face of God." . . .

Man will continue his conquest of space. To reach out for new goals and ever greater achievements—that is the way we shall commemorate our seven Challenger heroes.

—Ronald Reagan,
"Speech on the Challenger Disaster"
January 28, 1986

How a U.S. Secretary of State Stayed Bulletproof Under Fire

In 2002, Richard Ben-Veniste, a member of the Rogers Commission investigating 9/11, the worst act of domestic terrorism in U.S. history, grilled then U.S. National Security Adviser Dr. Condoleezza Rice on "what the President knew," and "when he knew it," in regard to the terrorists' plans for 9/11.

At the 9/11 hearing, Ben-Veniste's aim appeared to be to get Rice to answer those questions in a way that would show that President George W. Bush had prior intelligence regarding the impending attack and that he had failed to take adequate action to forestall it. If Ben-Veniste had succeeded, the political fallout for the President would have been devastating.

When you know you will face tough and ugly questions, and you know exactly what shape those tough and ugly questions will take, you need to be prepared for what's ahead.

Rice, who was later appointed Secretary of State, remained cool under repeated questioning. In fact, she ably defended her position, and that of President Bush. Let's analyze how she remained "bulletproof" under fire.

Secretary Rice knew Ben-Veniste would ask about the Presidential Daily Briefing (PDB) that Bush was given on August 6, 2001—just before the 9/11 attacks occurred. That PDB had been heavily redacted by President Bush's staff before being released to the public.

Because of that, many people believed the President had received a warning about an imminent attack on the United States, five weeks prior to 9/11, and then failed to act, and that his supporters or staff had redacted portions of the PDB to cover up the President's failure to act and respond appropriately.

So, knowing that Ben-Veniste was going to ask about the PDB, Secretary Rice prepared three **responses** to the anticipated hostile questions, as follows:
1. The PDB was a historical document.
2. There was nothing actionable in the PDB.
3. There were no new threats to pursue in the PDB.

Under questioning by Ben-Veniste, she stated and restated those positions. Collectively, in fact, she restated them *12 times* over a 15-minute time period.

Secretary Rice also offered some **viewpoints** about these positions. She used her viewpoints to further explain her support for these positions—but she always stuck to her three responses, and did so without wavering.

The result? Ben-Veniste was unable to get her to make a statement that opened President Bush to charges of nonfeasance, of failing to respond appropriately to a serious threat to national security.

Specifically, you need to pre-plan the positions you're going to take. Then you need to develop those and be able to expand on them. That was exactly what Secretary Rice did.

And you need more than one position, by the way. Think about it. Most issues and concerns are somewhat complex. They need to be approached from more than one angle. If you just keep repeating one position, or circling back to the same one, and are unable to articulate more than one argument to support your case, you may sound as if you have not been fully briefed. You also will fail to inspire confidence. Your aim is to present your information credibly and to inspire confidence, which is what happens when you prepare for this sort of questioning properly.

The Good News:

What They've Learned,

You Can Too

The good news is that great speakers and presenters and interviewees aren't born that way. Anyone who is a great communicator or presenter today is great because, somewhere along the line, he or she decided to go for it. They worked at developing their communication expertise. You can too.

Almost without exception, Fortune 500 CEOs are coached in public presenting at some point prior to being appointed to the C-Suite, and they continue to be coached—to polish their considerable skills— once they arrive in the C-Suite.

Even in belt-tightening times, corporations provide speech coaching to their up-and-coming managers. They know how vital it is for company leaders to excel at communication with the company's various audiences.

> "It usually takes me more than three weeks to
>
> prepare a good impromptu speech."
>
> —*Mark Twain*

If you have any doubts about the value of honing your communication skills consider this:

- **Preparation does make a difference**—Mitt Romney's huge win in the first Presidential Debate of 2012 was no accident. His staff announced that the candidate had been preparing for the October event since August. His debate performance *almost* turned around a campaign that, until that debate, had slumped badly. He fell behind again, and eventually lost, only after President Obama again found his footing as a strong debater. The unmistakable conclusion: debate performances and how well you do at the podium *do* matter.

- **Practice led to perfection**—Ronald Reagan developed his speaking voice as a radio announcer. He polished his oratorical skills during an eight-year stint serving as a spokesperson for GE Corporation. He gave 135 speeches during his tenure with GE, one at every GE plant.

- **Winston Churchill overcame a speech impediment**—Winston Churchill, one of the standout speakers of the 20th century, a man who changed history with his oratory, used to lisp. His doctor advised that "practice and perseverance" would enable him to overcome his speech impediment. Churchill went beyond mastering his lisp. He used his powerful oratory to enlist allies and assistance for his native land at a time when the stakes could not have been higher.

- **President Bill Clinton was booed early in his speaking career**—President Clinton, now widely considered among the best—if not *the* best—political speaker in the nation, was booed when he spoke at the 1988 Democratic National Convention. He wore out his welcome at the DNC when he spoke much longer than the 20 minutes he'd been allotted. Today, he is one of the very few speakers who can hold an audience at rapt attention, even for long speeches, as he proved at the 2012 Democratic National Convention. His speech there is widely credited with giving the incumbent President a strong boost in the polls.

(Search YouTube.com with the terms, "Clinton 1988 Democratic National Convention booed" to view the video.)

One executive at GE told anyone who led a presentation training program at GE to start the program with the quote below.

"When a young person comes in to present to me and he does well, I remember that, and the opposite is true too."

—Jack Welch, former CEO, GE

Jack Welch is not the only CEO to carefully scrutinize junior executives' communication skills. Anyone who demonstrates the potential to rise through the executive ranks will be expected to be a good one-to-group communicator.

So if you're going to be memorable when you present, be memorable on the positive side. Take the time to master communication skills. When opportunities arise to speak or present, take the time to prepare properly for each. The fact is, you never know who will be in the audience. Always prepare as if a key decision maker might decide to drop in—because that is exactly what could happen.

A note to the reader:
In the information we present in Chapters 2 through 4, you may feel we repeat certain concepts again and again. This repetition is intentional.

The chapters are organized as follows:
- *Chapter 2 outlines the elements of Executive Presence related to public speaking and presenting.*
- *Chapter 3 addresses the challenges we have observed hold speakers back from excelling at speaking and presenting.*

- *Chapter 4 takes you through two exercises proven to improve speaking and presenting skills. The Chapter 4 exercises enable you to apply what is presented in Chapter 2.*

In other words, in Chapters 2 through 4, each chapter builds on the previous chapter.

This is also the approach we bring to coaching speakers and presenters. We introduce the Executive Presence skill sets. Then, every time we coach, we build on those skill sets. We reinforce those skills, and add new ones.

2 – The Elements

of Executive Presence

- **What Is Executive Presence?**
- **The Elements of Executive Presence**
- **The Dr. Seuss Cure for a Flat Delivery**
- **Develop Your 'Speaker's Voice'**
- **Over the top? It Does Happen (but It's Rare)**
- **'But It Doesn't Feel Like Me," & The 4 Levels of Competency**

Anyone who aims to project leadership at the podium or when presenting to decision makers in a meeting needs to master the Executive Presence skill set.

What is Executive Presence?
Executive Presence is about how you look and how you sound to your business associates, colleagues and customers. When you have **Executive Presence**, you inspire confidence. The information you present or share is deemed trustworthy. You more effectively drive your organization's business results, and attract advancement and other opportunities.

The good news is, **Executive Presence** isn't some intangible quality gifted to a lucky few. Analyze leaders who exude it in public speaking

15

situations. You'll find it's made up of seven basic elements. Three are visual (what people see). Four are aural (what people hear).

As you adopt some of the Executive Presence "do this-es," they may feel uncomfortable to you initially. (See "But it doesn't feel like me" at the end of this chapter.) However, in very short order, what initially feels "not me" will become second nature to you as a presenter. Most important, these presentation skills will be "at the ready" when you need them, for that important meeting or for a presentation to a key client.

How were these determined? In 1970, Kevin Daley and Charlie Windhorst, pioneers in the executive coaching industry, undertook a revolutionary study and analysis of thousands of speakers and presenters. Using group feedback, they collected data on what worked, and what didn't work, to convey authority, credibility, confidence and passion—i.e., the intangibles of executive presence.

The end result? A specific body of observations that have since been successfully utilized by hundreds of thousands of Fortune 500 CEOs, senior leaders and sales executives both across the U.S., and across the world. The system developed by Kevin and Charlie has made it possible for struggling speakers to advance to effective levels, and for moderately effective speakers to communicate more powerfully. What's worked for them can work for you. So let's look at the visual elements of Executive Presence in public speaking.

The Elements

of Executive Presence

The 3 VISUAL Elements

EYES HANDS POSTURE

The 4 AURAL elements

VOLUME   INFLECTION

PACE   NON-WORDS

(ABSENCE OF)

*The **visual** elements of executive presence are determined by eyes, hands, and posture: where you look when you talk, how you position your hands and the gestures you make, and how you stand and move.*

Eyes

It is key to make eye contact with your audience—one person at a time. When you speak in front of a room, or seated at a meeting, you need to "gather your thought" (i.e., know what you are about to say), then look at one person, and maintain eye contact while saying that sentence or clause.

This moment of eyeball-to-eyeball connection and then of holding that connection is called **Focus.**

Think of plugging an electrical cord into a socket. Focus establishes the vital link between you and your audience.

When you finish your sentence, you pause. Holding the pause, you "gather your next thought." You may look down to your notes (if you need to do so). Then you find a new set of eyes and repeat the Focus process, as described above, with that person. Then you continue in this way throughout your speech or presentation: Each new thought is delivered to a fresh set of eyes.

The technique of Focus connects you with your audience, controls your pace, and keeps non-words ("ums," "ahs," etc.) at bay.

Avoid the temptation to "scan" the room—i.e., don't dart your eyes restlessly from one audience member to another. Complete a sentence or clause before breaking eye contact with one person and establishing it with another.

And, of course, don't stare down at your papers or technical equipment—your notes, speech text, index cards, PowerPoint screen, etc.—as you speak. Make eye contact with audience members.

Hands

Don't neglect to make use of your hands when you speak or present. Use them to gesture. Gestures make you more expressive. They add to your presentation. When you do gesture, remember to keep your hands completely open, and to gesture out away from your body, and up above your waist.

Here's why you want to avoid gesturing below your waist, at hip level—it's because the eye travels to flashes of light, color, and motion. That means your audiences' eyes will travel to your hands when they move. You want them looking at the upper half of your body—your face and your gestures.

Why is it preferable for you to gesture out to your sides? Again, the viewer's eye follows your movement. Movements out to your sides visually opens up your body, and make you come across as comfortable and engaging.

By the way, the "neutral position" (non-gesturing position) for an executive speaker/presenter is arms hanging at your sides and hands completely open. Why open hands? Remember, a hand offered in a handshake is fully open.

The open hand is a universal symbol of giving, trust and teamwork. Open hands make you look more approachable. Refrain from closing or clenching your hands, or from curling them into fists at your side. By the same token, don't clasp your hands in front of you, or behind.

Open hands reinforce the speaker's body language message of openness. For this reason, a speaker or presenter should avoid even cupping (semi-closing) his or her hands when speaking or presenting. In addition, when you use your hands to gesture, move your elbows out and away from your rib cage—i.e., avoid the Velcro effect. There should be "air" under your arms when you gesture.

Posture

That brings us to posture and movement. It's preferable you don't stand in one spot throughout your speech or presentation.

If you are standing behind a lectern, make an effort to step out from behind it once in a while. Is it essential to step out? No, and you may not want to do it until you advance in your speaking skills. But once you do begin to free yourself from behind the podium, it will add to the dynamism of your presentation.

When you do step forward, when speaking in front of a group, make sure to move in the direction of an audience member with whom you have made eye contact. When you arrive at your destination (a step or two away), complete your step by putting one foot next to the other to rebalance yourself. You need to end up with two feet solidly on the floor—not in an incomplete half-stepping position.

In other words, whenever you stop, your weight should be balanced "50-50." Why? A person who is visually balanced appears strong, confident, and in command—leadership qualities you want to project. Half-steps, and a hand on a hip, make a speaker appear visually asymmetrical. You no longer appear visually balanced.

If you move around when speaking, limit your movements. You don't want to move constantly. Nor should you rock back and forth, or right and left.

*Now let's look more closely at each of the **aural** elements of Executive Presence in public speaking—volume, inflection, pace and non-words (the absence of).*

Volume

Why is volume—specifically higher volume—important?

Two reasons.

- You want to ensure your listeners can hear you clearly.
- People who speak at a higher volume project confidence.

When people feel confident, they tend to speak more strongly (louder). We all know this, either on a conscious or unconscious level. So, when a speaker begins with a strong loud voice, listeners feel, "That speaker knows what he's talking about."

In other words, you easily and immediately accrue one of the characteristics of Executive Presence—credibility.

On a scale of 1 to 10, with one being a whisper, and 10 a shout, your "speaker's voice"—the voice you use when giving a speech or presentation—should be your voice at a 7–to-8 level. On the issue of volume, it's not uncommon for inexperienced speakers to say, "I'd be much better if I had a microphone." It's a resourceful thought, but—interestingly—it's simply not true.

A mike can't cure "the mumbles." It can make you louder— but not less boring.

A speaker who has not learned to project his or her voice by upping the volume *naturally* sounds just as uninspiring with a mike as without one. Yes, you can make your voice *sound* louder with technology, but you can't take the "boring" out that way. A poor speaker with a mike amplifying a subdued tentative voice will be just as dull as when he spoke without the benefit of wires and amplifiers.

Why? To answer that, let's look at the second aural element of Executive Presence—*inflection*.

Inflection

When you speak, it's natural for you to say *some* of the words and phrases in a sentence—but never *each* word in a sentence—louder or softer. Inflection refers to those "peaks and valleys" in your speaker's voice.

Since we've lain in the crib and taken in the world—even before we understood what words meant—we learned that people emphasize the *important* words. And they emphasize them by saying them more loudly—or more softly.

People signal

the important words

by *inflecting* them.

So, a speaker or presenter needs to inflect the key points in the messages he or she delivers. If they fail to do that, two things happen:
1. Listeners *struggle to hear* the speaker. (An uninflected voice is heard as a drone, a soft buzz. More than anything else, it induces sleep.
2. Listeners will mentally tag the speaker or presenter "boring"—*not* a characteristic of Executive Presence.

Try this exercise—Read the Gettysburg Address *without inflecting a single word*. Actually this is difficult to do.

THE GETTYSBURG ADDRESS (EXCERPT)

The world will little note, nor long remember what we say here, but it can never forget what they did here. It is for us the living, rather, to be dedicated here to the unfinished work which they who fought here have thus far so nobly advanced. It is rather for us to be here dedicated to the great task remaining before us—that . . . government of the people, by the people, for the people, shall not perish from the earth.

— Abraham Lincoln, Nov. 19, 1863

The words themselves are so moving, they *beg* to be inflected. But try this exercise and you will hear how an uninflected delivery manages to diminish even the power of words deeply imbued with feeling.

On the other hand, inflect a meaningless sentence—say, Lewis Carroll's "Twas brillig and the slithy toves, etc." (See below.)

JABBERWOCKY (EXCERPT)

'Twas brillig, and the slithy toves

Did gyre and gimble in the wabe:

All mimsy were the borogoves,

And the mome raths outgrabe.

—Lewis Carroll, *Through the Looking-Glass*

& What Alice Found There

Or try, "The quick brown fox jumps over the lazy dog." You will "hear" how an inflected delivery has the potential to attract an audience. That's because it's the intensity of the feeling a speaker projects that attracts audiences.

The absence of inflection equals a flat (emotionless) delivery. The emotion connecting the speaker to the audience disappears. Listeners blank out.

There are only four things a speaker can do with her voice:
1. She can raise it or lower it (volume and inflection).
2. She can speed it up or slow it down (pace).

That's it. But speakers working with those four options have delivered speeches that have changed the world.

THE DR. SEUSS CURE FOR A FLAT DELIVERY

A great way to practice inflection is with a child's book. Get hold of a picture book and read out loud from it. Imagine you are reading to a small child— a child whose attention you need to keep. That means you will try to bring the words and pictures to life for the child. (*Oh, the Places You'll Go!* by Dr. Seuss is a good book for this exercise. Often given as a graduation gift, it contains a meaningful message for adults, while also being an enjoyable book for children.)

All of us naturally inflect the sentences we read to our children (or grandchildren, as the case may be). We naturally put enthusiasm into our delivery. We naturally draw out key passages. We might point to the pictures, but we also deliver "special effects" vocally. All of these rhetorical effects come naturally to us when we read to a child.

The children's book exercise will help drive out

any flatness in your speeches. When you actually

give a speech or presentation, you won't inflect as

much as you do when you read a child's book out

loud. *But* if you've had a tendency toward flat

delivery, and you learn to move in the storybook

delivery direction, audiences will find your

speeches suddenly have more sparkle—and they

will be "stickier" (more memorable) as well.

Wait a minute, you might think—does emotion have any place in the business world? Isn't it all supposed to be about facts, figures, and the bottom line?

Yes and no. Yes, facts and results are what matter at the end of the day. But results are driven by feelings—more specifically by messages delivered with feeling.

It's considered a compliment in business circles, after all, to be thought of as intense and passionate—about your work, and about results. Attend a stockholders meeting sometime when the bottom line isn't doing so well. Emotionless? Not quite.

So, yes, emotion—directed at the tasks at hand—has its place in the business world. And it definitely has a place in your speeches and presentations. The more passion you bring to your topic, the more likely you are to connect with your audience in a powerful way. And when you do that, your audience is more likely to heed your "believe this," "know this," or "do this" messages.

Pace

Q. What is the right pace for a speaker?

A. The pace that holds an audience's interest.

Just as you can speak louder or softer (inflection), so too, you can speak more quickly or more slowly. This is your **Pace**.

The *pace* at which you speak provides you with a third element for building your Executive Presence.

Many speakers are criticized for speaking too fast. When this happens listeners feel the speaker is racing through his sentences.

They have difficulty following the speaker from one thought to another and believe it is because of a too-rapid delivery.

In fact, very few speakers actually do speak *too fast*. What usually happens in these cases is that a speaker fails to *pause* at the end of a thought.

In effect, he fails to create those tiny breaks in his speech that listeners need in order to absorb what he has just told them.

When you eliminate pauses in a speech, your listeners will still be trying to digest one thought as you are racing through the next. Result: your messages have a harder time getting through. And, of course, you fail to establish Executive Presence. When you race through a speech this way, you are talking *at* your audience, not *to* them. You miss the opportunity to connect.

A good speaker not only builds pauses into his delivery. He also will occasionally vary his pace—both for dramatic effect, and to enhance the "stickiness" of his speech.

It's easy to vary your pace. On occasion, simply slow down—or speed up—when you deliver a key sentence or clause in your speech. In other words, build some play into your delivery. Vary your pace and you prevent your speech from becoming ponderous.

> # The four great non-words
> # in American English
> # are
> # "Um" "Uh" "Like" "You know"—
> ### *Polished speakers avoid the above.*

Non-words

(absence of)

As a leader, your goal is to appear powerful, confident, enthusiastic, and dynamic when you speak—all attributes we associate with Executive Presence. Be wary, then, of the non-words ("um," "uh," "like," and "you know").

When a speaker drops "ums" or "uhs,"—the non-words—it's usually when he's completed a thought and is transitioning to the next.

An occasional non-word won't sink you—although it's best to eliminate them completely, if you can.

The problem with "ums" and "uhs" is they make a speaker sound weak, tentative and slow. It sounds as if you're reaching for the next thought—with difficulty.

This effect is the opposite of powerful and confident.

Here's something handy to remember: Next time you listen to a speaker who is dropping non-words, take the time to observe *when* it happens. You'll find a speaker gushes non-words when he looks down or at the floor, or up at the ceiling. It almost never happens when a speaker makes or maintains eye contact with an audience member. And it's almost always on the transition from one thought to the next or from one sentence to the next. You'll find this is very consistent.

So train yourself to deliver your speeches and presentations using **Focus**, an easy-to-master technique that ensures you maintain eye contact with the audience.

> *Note:* In Chapter 4, we present the above outlined elements of Executive Presence in handy "do's" and "don'ts" format.

Develop your

'speaker's voice'

Business leaders new to public speaking sometimes balk at the idea of developing a "speaker's voice." This is because each of us feels we have a "natural" voice we use to speak to others.

It's true that each of us has a voice we use comfortably in non-formal communication. Our "everyday" voice serves us perfectly well day to day. But that voice—the one we use to communicate to family members, friends, and colleagues one-to-one—may very well be a detriment if it's the voice we use for business presentations.

In public speaking, you need to develop your "one-to-group" diction, also known as your "speaker's voice."

You need to set aside your "normal" (one-to-one) voice or diction when you address an audience or present at a meeting.

As you begin to take on more and more public speaking, work to consciously develop your public speaking voice (your one-to-group voice).

So how do you develop your one-to-group voice?

Simple. You take your one-to-one voice and push its boundaries. When you're "on"—delivering messages to a group—adjust your volume. Take it to a 7-to-8 level. (See the sections on Volume, Inflection, and Pace earlier in this chapter.) Inflect important words. Use pace so as to hold an audience's attention.

SPEECHES REQUIRE

YOUR 'SPEAKER'S VOICE'

Diction (also known as "enunciation") =

the qualities of a speaker's voice that

make it distinctive, including inflection,

accent, and volume.

Why should you work to develop a "speaker's voice"?

Because the quality of your voice when you give a speech or presentation largely determines whether you successfully project Executive Presence in your speeches and presentations, or whether you fail to do so.

When you use your untrained one-to-one voice addressing a group, you diminish your vocal energy. When you use what you know about volume, inflection and pace—i.e., use your speaker's voice—your Executive Presence increases.

Is your one-to-group voice, your speaker's voice, somehow artificial or "phony"?

Not at all. In fact, you need to be genuine, one-to-group. But there is nothing insincere about using your speaker's voice.

Taking care to develop your speaker's voice is part of business etiquette. You are being thoughtful of, and respectful to, your audiences. You are making it as easy as possible for listeners to absorb your messages painlessly and even *enjoyably*.

Kevin Daley, founder of Communispond—the company that established the industry of executive speech coaching—recalls that once he had taken the training, one Fortune 500 CEO refused to listen to any internal presentations unless the presenter had received executive presentation training.

In that sense, taking the time to develop your speaker's voice is a gauge of your stewardship to the organization you serve.

By developing an effective public speaking voice, you increase your value to the organization, as well as your effectiveness in serving its interests.

There is nothing phony

or artificial

about developing

your speaker's voice.

Your speaker's voice will be "something new" to you initially. But don't confuse "new" with "artificial." The "newness" will fade. As you become accustomed to using your one-to-group diction, it will begin to feel natural. When business leaders first begin practicing one-to-group diction, most err on the side of thinking, "I'm being too theatrical (or too dynamic, or too loud)."

And that isn't the case. In fact, it's quite the opposite.

Over the top?

It does happen

(but it's rare)

Speakers rarely go "over the top." But in a 2005 speech, Microsoft Chairman Steve Ballmer became an exception. To begin his speech, he bounded onto the podium, leaping around and screaming, "Give it up," to the audience at the top of his lungs. The video of this episode went viral, and has garnered over four million hits on YouTube.com at this writing.

(Enter the search words "Steve Ballmer" on YouTube.com to view the video.)

Ballmer provides a vivid example of Too Much. But the fact that the video capture went viral also underscores how very rare it is for a public speaker to actually go too far in the overemphatic direction. The few who actually do go overboard get a *lot* of attention exactly because they are so exceptional.

Dealing with "But it doesn't feel like me"
Will the body language and vocal energy you need to project at the podium—or at a meeting—feel natural to you?

Yes and no. Once you have mastered the skills and begin to use them consistently, they *will* become second nature to you. Initially, you may feel the way you did when you first learned how to golf or play tennis. The swings and stances that would later enable you to be at the top of your game weren't "natural" at first. But, as you mastered them, and used them consistently, they became "you" as a golfer or "you" as a tennis player.

Once you master and become familiar with the Executive Presence skill set the skills will become "you" as a speaker and a presenter.

Do you use the skills at the breakfast table or in the coffee break room?

No. You use the skills when "you're on." At other times—in social situations and casual interactions—at ease, soldier.

95% of all speakers

need to project

more energy.

In all of the considerable time I have coached speakers, I've only once had to suggest that a presenter "dial it down."

– John M. Vautier

"But it doesn't feel like me"

& the 4 Levels of Competency

With any physical skill (versus an intellectual skill), each of us advances through 4 levels of competency:

1. Unconscious Incompetence
2. Conscious Incompetence
3. Conscious Competence
4. Unconscious Competence

As an example, let's use ice skating.

1. *Unconscious Incompetence*

As a child, I watch my brother and sister put their ice skates on, step out onto the ice and skate away. And *I think, "That looks easy, I can do that." (I have Unconscious Incompetence.)*

2. *Conscious Incompetence*

Mom puts the skates on my feet and now I can't even stand up. *(Now I have Conscious Incompetence. I'm aware that ice skating is not as easy as my brother and sister made it look.)*

3. *Conscious Competence*

If you take your kids to an ice rink to learn to skate today, they will most likely be taught to master the ice by being given one of the orange road cones we see along the highways to hold onto as they venture onto the ice in their hockey skates. Imagine a five-year-old in this situation. The coach tells him, "Grab the top of the cone and push it across the ice." This gets the newbie skater to move forward on his skates. If he wobbles, the cone keeps him upright even if his legs are shaky. The newbie skater then is instructed to step forward with the right foot and then to push that foot back to move the cone forward, and then to do the same with the left foot. Slowly but surely his body masters the motions needed to skate without depending on the cone. *(This is the beginning of Conscious Competence.)*

4. *Unconscious Competence*

After the newbie has practiced long enough with the cone, he eventually can step out onto the ice and skate away. *(The newbie skater now has Unconscious Competence.)*

The mind has not trained the body to master ice skating in the process above. The body has trained the mind. The physical elements of effective public speaking may feel as new and strange as ice does to a newbie skater at first. But practice and experience will just as surely result in mastery.

"But it doesn't feel like me."

Many times in a coaching session a client will say, "This doesn't feel natural at all," or "Harry doesn't look natural doing what you just coached him to do."

We ask the client if *we* look and sound natural when we do it. Most of the time we get a yes response. Then we explain that this is the difference between Conscious and Unconscious Competence.

In Conscious Competence a person is still "consciously" working on each skill. At this stage, it doesn't always feel or look natural.

 A newbie golfer who picks up a golf club for the first time will hold it the way you'd hold a baseball bat, one hand above the other. Then someone comes along and says, "No, no. You take your pinky on your lower hand and you take your index finger from your upper hand and link them together as you grab the grip of the club."

And the newbie's first reaction is, "You've got to be kidding me." No way. I can't hit that ball holding the club that way."

But that is the correct grip. And, over time, it begins to feel natural.

It's the same with the Executive Presence skills. You'll find that as you move from Conscious Competence to Unconscious Competence, you progressively look and feel more comfortable.

Speakers and presenters who master the skills, as anyone who puts in the time and effort can do, look good at what they do. They make it look easy.

Note: Of the Executive Presence skills, the most challenging skill to take to the Unconscious Competence level is Focus (looking at one person as you present one thought). Over time, speakers can get close to Unconscious Competence with Focus, but it still may not feel totally natural.

The other skills—involving hands, posture, gestures, movement, volume, and inflection—all more quickly begin to seem natural when the "you're on" moments happen. And, to an audience, they look natural.

But with Focus (the use of the eyes), a speaker may continue to need to consciously remember to do it. When speakers finally take Focus to the Unconscious Competence level, they often refer to it as being "in The Zone."

Executive Presence results when you master a skill set

Bottom line

Executive Presence doesn't just happen. It is a skill you work to acquire. Just as you learn to hold a meeting, or manage your cash flow in order to succeed in business, so too you need to acquire the Executive Presence skill set to utilize when you speak or present.

The skills are not complex, but mastery requires a commitment to the process and discipline in applying the skill set.

3 – Why Comfort Is Optional

- Public Speaking Is the Best Way to Boost Visibility
- But I'm Doing Just Fine, Aren't I?
- Face Up to Your Borgs
- What the Boston Marathon Teaches Speakers
- You're Not in This Alone (At Least, You Don't Have to Be)

Why should you make public speaking one of your priorities?
Because nothing builds careers like positive visibility. Public speaking is one of the best ways to gain that visibility. It puts you in the direct line of sight of audiences ranging from fellow employees, to C-Suite executives, to stockholders, to clients, to university and college students, to staff, to the media, to the general public, and to decision makers of all shapes and sizes.

Skillful Public Speaking =

Positive Visibility =

Career Growth

Even a minimal amount of effort will ensure you become a competent speaker. Serious effort on your part will elevate you to the next level among executive speakers. And it's no accident that executives deemed "hot properties" also usually fall into the "sought after" speaker category.

But I'm doing just fine, aren't I?
Avoid the temptation to coast. Some leaders today might be tempted to think: "I don't really need to hone my formal speaking skills. I won't ever need to give a formal speech or presentation. Almost all my key presentations are delivered sitting in conference rooms."

It's true that we're seeing a huge migration across business America to seated presentations in conference room settings. Often these involve distributing handouts and then explaining the handouts. What could be easier?

Public Speaking

Is the Best Way

To Boost Visibility

A faulty conclusion is drawn: "I only need enough of a skill set to squeak by when presenting in a conference room setting."

But if you limit your skill set this way, you cap your Executive Presence potential and we can guarantee that you are setting yourself up for a painful wake-up call at some point in the future.

Sure, if you are usually called upon to deliver a presentation in what has become a comfortable setting (seated among colleagues), you begin to feel you deliver very well. You even begin to feel that if you're called upon someday to deliver in front of a room—as will inevitably happen—you'll transfer those delivery skills you've "honed" seated at a conference table to "front of the room" presentations and do just fine.

But when you finally find yourself standing in front of a group versus sitting around a table with the same group, here's what happens: You discover that the skill set required is higher.

Why? Because your comfort level changes when you're standing in front of a room. It's more challenging to deliver to a group when you're standing facing them. That's because delivering well in front of a group demands more from a speaker/presenter.

And if you falter and stumble your first time up, you can seriously erode the Executive Presence capital you've banked to date.

If you've mastered the art of how to deliver well when standing in front of a room, you also are guaranteed to be a strong presenter when seated at a table. However, the reverse is not true.

A speaker abruptly called upon to present standing in front of a group (versus seated with the group) feels vulnerable. The resulting body language says it all. "Fight or flight" instincts take over. Untrained speakers often put a hand on a hip (feisty). Or they hug themselves (defensive body language), or they hold their arms down and clasp their hands in front of themselves (fig leaf position—also defensive). Even if a speaker also feels "fight or flight" emotions when seated, her anxiety is masked visually. When you're seated, a smaller area of you is visible. Your audience doesn't see that much of you. So they miss the legs crossing (defensive), or the toe tapping (agitation) because it's masked.

In addition, when you present seated, you are more physically constrained. That is because of the natural tendency not to invade your seated neighbors' space. Your movements are just smaller. So, whatever you do, movement-wise, has less impact. Your movements, when you present in front of a room, should be different from what they are when you are seated—your movements should be larger and tailored to presenting while standing. But if you never train for the eventuality, you are almost sure to flounder first time up.

Get *in front of the room* and no one is going to miss the body language when the body language fails you—as when your hands take the fig leaf/folded arms position, when you cross one leg over the other (defensive), when you shift your weight to one hip (lack of confidence), when you make a half-step forward, then retreat back (uncertainty), or when there is constant movement (agitation).

Your body language,

in front of a room,

speaks volumes about your

Executive Presence—

or the lack thereof.

Bottom line: Your body language sends signals—and the signals are more visible and more highlighted when you are standing front and center before a group of listeners. A table is no longer there to mute the display.

Vautier's Words to the Wise

No one will spend his entire career giving speeches or presentations from a seat at a table. A business person on his way up—at some point in his career—will have to stand (in front of the room) and deliver.

And at some point in his career, he also will have to make a formal presentation. It could be very short. It could be from notes. It might be behind a lectern—or without one. But it *will* be formal and it *will* be in front of the room. And the speaker/ presenter needs to be able to avoid fumbling and stumbling.

Leaders need to hone communication skills

As a leader, your ability to communicate well, and to convey Executive Presence, is always a matter for consideration and judgment. Few executives move very far up the ladder if they fail to convince decision makers that they have the Right Stuff when it comes to communicating on behalf of the company.

Given the benefits, why do some leaders drag their feet when it comes to mastering public speaking?

People make certain action items a priority only when they realize the importance of those action items. Often a young executive manages to advance in his career without giving a major speech or presentation. Busy with the many responsibilities that fall on any capable leader's to-do list, the executive may put off scheduling time to advance his communication skills.

But then, inevitably, he is invited to deliver a major speech or an important presentation.

At that point, a scramble ensues to prep for this event. A speechwriter is located. A coach is enlisted. Time is siphoned from other pressing initiatives. The executive's anxiety level rises as it becomes clear he must devote more hours than he realized would be necessary to prepare for this event—and his calendar, as is usually the case, has little breathing room. The scramble and the hectic pace could have been avoided.

As soon as it is clear you are headed for increased responsibilities, begin working on your speaking and presenting skills.

Face Up to Your Borgs

In the TV series *Star Trek: The Next Generation*, the Borg—enemies of mankind—are fond of saying, "Resistance is futile."

Of course, resistance actually isn't futile for the heroes of *Star Trek*, who always find a way to resist the evil plans of the Borg.

However, in the business world resistance *is* futile—that is, when it comes to mastering presentation skills. You do yourself a disservice when you put off working on this key skill. The idea of getting up in front of your peers and bosses and of presenting at meetings, can be daunting. But, if you intend to advance in your career, you need to face up to your "Borgs."

The good news is:

- Once you start to master communication techniques and gain experience in public presenting and speaking, you'll discover that if you work at your skills and prepare properly for speaking events, you truly have nothing to fear.
- You also will learn that while you may not be comfortable, at first, as a speaker or a presenter, you can do an excellent job and impress your boss and your peers anyway. The trick is to *appear* comfortable—and that is something you can do. This book will help.

Audiences view

confident speakers

as capable leaders.

A few words on "comfort"

I often ask people I coach, "How would you like people to describe you as a speaker or presenter? What is the adjective or adverb you believe would mean your speech or presentation went pretty well?" The answer I most often hear is: "Comfortable." They want to appear at ease and relaxed to their listeners.

This is understandable. If someone comes across to us as nervous or rattled (the opposite of "comfortable") when he/she presents, we may be sympathetic. But we downgrade our opinion of the presenter's professionalism. They fail to deliver an aura of "mastery."

On the other hand, we automatically elevate our opinion of speakers and presenters who articulate their messages clearly and who appear confident ("comfortable"). That's because most of us have observed that people who are experts in their fields tend to be at ease when they speak publicly.

The hard truth is,

it doesn't matter

if you're comfortable;

you only need to

look and *sound* comfortable.

DO YOU NEED TO BE COMFORTABLE? The hard truth of it is, it doesn't matter if you're comfortable. Of course, it would be nice if you always felt comfortable when you presented. But what's really important is that you *look* and *sound* comfortable—and that's what I intend to help you do. This book will provide you with techniques to project confidence—no matter how you actually feel.

YOU ONLY NEED TO *APPEAR* AT EASE. Because when you *appear* to be comfortable, other people will accept that you *are*. They won't *know* if you feel insecure and nervous.

YOU CAN LEARN HOW TO APPEAR COMFORTABLE. In this book, I intend to provide you with the knowledge and techniques you need to enable you to present as the comfortable, natural, genuine, sincere speaker your audiences want to hear—even early in your speaking and presenting efforts.

What the Boston Marathon Teaches Speakers

Marathon runners have a certain stride they can maintain with ease. But sometimes, as in the Boston Marathon, the terrain varies. It goes from flat to hilly. When this happens, the challenge runners face literally becomes steeper.

For a runner the flat terrain is routine, but the hills—the more challenging non-routine segments—are "spikes." A runner who trains regularly handles spikes with ease. Routine running builds the muscles and stamina needed to make an extra effort.

So too, even after you become a capable speaker, there are times when the message you need to deliver will be more challenging. At those times, you may—for one reason or another—feel less comfortable than usual. You may find you need to make an extra effort. Discomfort doesn't mean you will present less than ably— provided you prepare properly. This book will present how to's that will help with any situation you face as an executive communicator.

Discomfort—Make It Work to Your Advantage

Anxiety often spikes a flow of adrenaline. If you don't control the anxiety, it can:

- close off your speaking voice
- make you shrink and use defensive body language
- make you small or quiet

> **Most speakers relax & find their stride**
>
> **3 minutes into a speech.**

Vautier's Words to the Wise: Take All the Opportunities To Speak Your Schedule Allows

If you lack confidence as a presenter at the moment, be patient with yourself. Your initial goal is to look and sound comfortable. Over time, with experience, as you rack up your "lectern time," you'll find yourself growing more and more comfortable as a speaker. As you advance in your career, you will be presented with increasing opportunities to speak and to present— both internally and externally. Grab these opportunities.

As you gain experience as a speaker, you will internalize the sense that, "I can get up and do this, and I can do it any time I need to—even on a day-to-day basis"—i.e., you will grow increasingly at ease when communicating to audiences. You will also gain a reputation as the "go-to communicator"—the leader who is willing to step up and present ably. This will lead to your increased visibility—and will attract more opportunities for you.

Keep this in mind: Discomfort is not always a bad thing. In fact, speakers who are a little too complacent can come across as flat. *A certain amount of adrenaline drives us to do our best, and bolsters us as we undertake a new challenge.* The idea is for you to control the adrenaline bump, versus letting *it* control *you*. This book will teach you the techniques to do that. It will enable you to *own* your speaking opportunity, to take charge of yourself and of the situation.

You're Not in This Alone
(At Least, You Don't Have to Be)

Should you get professional communications training? Do you really need a coach? Can't you just read the tips provided in this book and make do?

To the last point, yes, this book will enable you to advance your skills beyond where they were at your starting point. Read, absorb, and practice the skills outlined, and you will be far ahead of colleagues and competitors who fail to make any effort to polish their public speaking and presentation skills.

Why seek out a coach to learn how to talk?

We're all born talking. It's no big deal, right?

Well, it *is* a big deal *when you don't do it well*.

But professional coaching will speed your learning curve. Without the skilled and objective feedback a good coach provides, it can be easy for you to miss problem areas longer than you need to—not to mention missing the solutions. A professional coach can point these out to you—tactfully and effectively—in short order.

In addition—to truly practice speaking and presentation skills—which you will need to do to master them, it is best to be in a setting that approaches a "real world" scenario as much as possible—something a coach will arrange.

A coach should always videotape your presentations (exercises) so that he can provide you with "instant playback" critiques. This is one of the most effective ways for newbie speakers to learn mastery, and for more advanced speakers to further polish their skills. A coach also will arrange exercises in a sequence that makes the important "do's" and "don'ts" of public speaking make sense for you. In short, good coaching will speed your learning curve.

Why would a business leader *not* seek coaching to acquire this skill so critical to success in the business world?

In other words, a good coach structures each practice session to focus on a key skill, in an audience environment, while providing "instant replay" feedback.

That's why coaching is the best and most efficient way to master speaking and presentation skills. Unfortunately, it is impossible to duplicate all of these benefits on a do-it-yourself basis. But why should you?

If you have children who aim to compete for a place in their school's tennis/swim/basketball/golf or other teams, how likely are you to enlist a coach's assistance to help them prepare for the pre-tryouts and tryouts? Of course, you'll sign them up for coaching sessions.

My wife and I invested a sizable sum for coaching for each of our three children to help them make their junior high basketball teams. And it helped them succeed.

The amount parents spend for sports, arts, and music coaching for their children—not to mention coaching for ACT tests—is phenomenal. As parents we want our kids to do well—and we're willing to invest in their success.

Athletes, whether newbies or pros, also know the value of coaching. Any business leader who needs to bring his public speaking skills up to par with what is expected of today's business leaders is similar to a pro athlete who needs to work on some aspect of his sport.

Why would a business leader committed to providing his organi- zation with his best efforts *not* seek coaching to acquire this skill so critical to success in the business world? Why would anyone think to aim at the executive suite, and not seek out professional help?

Certainly you are not likely to meet resistance within your organization. Human Resources departments are four-square behind leadership communication coaching.

Talent management is now a very strong focus for most companies. Today, companies that carefully watch the bottom line still make it a priority to invest in developing new talent—and the talent they have.

The talent management teams at major corporations—the Human Resources specialists who identify, develop, and polish new talent, and who refine the abilities of seasoned employees—recognize the importance of training leaders to communicate ably on behalf of their organizations.

Even during the last recession, when coaching in the soft skills was a hard sell to belt-tightening corporations, companies with their belts pulled tight still budgeted funds to train their leadership talent in public speaking and presentation skills.

Outstanding organizations, like the University of Pittsburgh Medical Center and Allstate exercise two talent-training arms—one for new hires, fresh out of school, and one for longer-standing employees who have advanced to positions where they and the company will benefit from honing their communication skills. Investing in new— and in existing—talent in this way has a payoff in employee retention. Companies that invest in developing their employees' communications capacities demonstrate that they are in the forefront. And employees who feel they are part of a forward-thinking organization—one "with its act together" and that views them as valuable assets—tend to remain loyal to their employers.

It was my privilege to coach four of the last six CEOs at Ford Motor Company. I coached one of them, Alex Trotman, from the time he was a rising star with Ford of Europe, up through his tenure as CEO of Ford. Alex knew the value of excellence in public speaking. No one was more committed than he was to ensuring he would consistently give his all as a speaker.

I first met him when I coached him as part of a group of talented young Ford of Europe executives. He appreciated the training offered and quickly mastered the nuances. When he became Ford's CEO, he asked me to let him know when I planned to visit Detroit, and said he would set aside 15 or 20 minutes at those times to fine-tune his skills. And that was exactly what he did. I would meet him for a coaching session once or twice a year for the five years he oversaw Ford as CEO.

It was important to him to continuously improve as an executive communicator—and he did improve. People who knew him often commented on his down-to-earth quality. In fact, when filmmaker Michael Moore—hoping to prove that Detroit's auto CEOs were out of touch with their products—challenged Alex to change the oil on one of Ford's SUVs, the CEO donned a pair of overalls and did exactly that. He took the same practical approach to advancing his mastery of executive communications.

He knew it was a skill that could be fine-tuned, that if you took the time to practice you could only get better and better—and he did.

Vautier's Words to the Wise:

Breathe!

One simple technique for overriding an adrenaline spike is to simply breathe deeply into your abdomen. Deep abdominal breathing is a natural tranquilizer. If you need to do it at the podium, before your presentation, go ahead. Take three slow deep breaths. No one can tell, and it has the added benefit of providing you with a dramatic pause—a great set-up for your opening sentence.

It's also useful to know that, about two or three minutes into a speech or presentation, most people find their stride. The adrenalin burn is played through. You relax and it's easier sailing from there.

4 - What a Difference a Day (or Two) of Coaching Makes

- Costas, David Letterman, & 'The Fridge'
- Focus: What the Fridge Learned & What You Can Too
- The 3 Kinds of Sentences & Real-World Communication
- Why You Should Avoid the 'Fig Leaf Position': or, the Do's and Don'ts of Executive Presence
- The 3 Levels of Engagement

Costas, David Letterman, & 'The Fridge'

Early in my career, I was fortunate enough to have had the opportunity to coach William Perry ("The Fridge"). This was when his star had just begun to rise. It was clear from the start that Perry would be a football great—if he didn't get hurt—because he was a fantastic player.

But then a segment aired on TV that fall. In it, sportscaster Bob Costas interviewed Perry at Soldier Field. The TV segment made it clear to me, and others, that The Fridge needed another kind of coaching—coaching that had nothing to do with football.

Here's what happened on the TV segment: Costas thrust the mike in Perry's face and interviewed him. Responding to the questions, the Fridge must have said "um" at least 15 times—in 15 seconds. As a result, he sounded unsure of himself—a poor communicator. The reason this mattered was that Perry was poised to be tapped for highly lucrative endorsement deals—part of the territory for a sports superstar. But to cement those deals he needed to come across as a poised—and articulate—professional. One thing was clear: He had been given no preparation for the media assault ahead.

Through my contacts, I reached his agent and I offered to provide coaching. The agent told me that Perry was scheduled to do an interview on *Late Night with David Letterman* in a week's time. He also told me that, yes, he'd been flooded with endorsement offers for Perry—but he knew they could vanish as quickly as they materialized if his client made a serious misstep on Letterman's show.

Given Letterman's capacity for needling humor, the agent was particularly concerned that The Fridge be coached on how to handle any jokes lobbed at him at his expense. (No matter how attractive a sports figure may be, advertisers have little interest in celebrities with short fuses.)

I signed on to prep The Fridge for the Letterman show, and I had two sessions with him. I helped him prepare for any tough or needling questions and we worked on eliminating non-words, like "um" and "you know." (I later learned that one group of sportswriters had a pool going on how many times The Fridge was going to say "you know" during his Letterman interview.)

The long and short of it was, The Fridge did a great job on Letterman's show. Letterman couldn't have been nicer to him. The two of them got along terrifically well. The Fridge came across as the likable personality he was. He did use a few non-words, but they were minimal and truly not noticeable. Compared to his performance in the Costas interview, it was night and day.

Focus:

What 'The Fridge' learned

& what you can too

Step One:

The 7th Inning Stretch,

or How to Focus

(an Audience's Attention)

This exercise is as simple as the 7th Inning Stretch that is a ritual in many ball parks, including my favorite—Wrigley Field. But simple as it is, it's also powerful. Why? It lays the basis for your success as a speaker and presenter. See the next page for how to do it.

The 7ᵗʰ Inning Stretch Exercise (Focus)

Locate a meeting room you can have to yourself for the half hour or so you practice this exercise.

Line up eight or more chairs that will face you as you stand in the front of the room. They can be arranged in a single or double row. (It's even better if you can round up eight people willing to play audience. If you can't, just imagine people seated in those chairs and imagine making eye contact with them in the exercise below.)

Review the first eight lines of "Take Me Out to the Ball Game." (See below.) If you need to, read the lines from the next page of this book.

Now, recite the lyrics in the following way:

- Gather the first line of "Ball Game" in your mind. Then look at one person in your audience. Make eye contact with that person.
- Looking at that person, say, "Take me out to the ball game." Maintain eye contact with that person until you finish saying that whole first sentence.

- Look down at your "notes." Gather the next line. Allow a "beat" or two of silence. This is the pause.
- Then look at another "person" in the "audience." Make eye contact.
- Now say the next line: "Take me out to the crowd." Maintain eye contact with the second person until you finish that whole second sentence.
- Repeat this with the remaining six lines.

> *Take me out to the ball game,*
>
> *Take me out with the crowd;*
>
> *Buy me some peanuts and Cracker Jack,*
>
> *I don't care if I never get back.*
>
> *Let me root, root, root for the home team,*
>
> *If they don't win, it's a shame.*
>
> *For it's one, two, three strikes, you're out,*
>
> *At the old ball game.*

Note: Switch around your eye contact. Don't proceed to make eye contact chair by chair, left to right, or vice versa. That would come across as odd and mechanical. Rather, look at one audience member, somewhere left of center. Then at an audience member somewhere right of center. then somewhere close to the center. Switch it around in a non-mechanical rhythm—left, right, center / right, left, center / left, center, right, or other variations.

What does this exercise help you master?

The idea is:

- You have eight thoughts expressed in eight simple sentences (your content).
- You connect with one listener to express one thought.
- Then you move on to another listener to express the next thought. And so on.
- Delivering your content this way, you are forced to replace "ums" and "uhs" with a pause—i.e., you eliminate the "non-words."

By the way, a practice speech text that contains only three thoughts (sentences) will be too short to do this exercise. That's because it doesn't allow you to get into the routine of delivering one complete thought to one pair of eyes enough times to get a feel for the natural rhythm of effective speech delivery.

If you look at someone in the audience,

someone you're presenting to, and

maintain eye contact for the duration of a

complete thought you are expressing,

your credibility goes up. You come

across as a strong, confident, credible

speaker—as someone who has mastery

of her material.

Why do you have to deliver a complete thought to one set of eyes? Because it prevents you from scanning an audience—that is, delivering one thought while running your eyes over several sets of eyes. When you "scan" an audience—let your eyes skim over the people listening to you—like a pebble skimming across the water—you come across as less confident and credible.

The "scanning" also is subtly off-putting to your audience. It's as if you do not trust any individual member of the audience to "get" your message—or as if you are reluctant to establish the momentary intimacy with any particular listener that this short duration of eye contact allows. Scanning can make you appear to be impatient—or wishing you were elsewhere. Bottom line, when you scan, you fail to engage your audience; you miss the opportunity to connect.

The "Ball Park" method of maintaining eye contact *forces* you to engage your audience.

The first step of engagement with another human being is eye contact. And when was the last time you saw an audience member look down at his smart phone when a public speaker was making eye contact with him?

The 7th Inning Stretch Exercise Grounds You in the Base Skill of Focus

To recap, the process is:
- Make eye contact with an audience member, and state a single thought to that person.
- Pause. Gather your next thought. (Look down at your notes to do so, if needed.) Make eye contact with another audience member.
- Speak a new thought to that new pair of eyes.
- Rinse and repeat, eight times. (Okay, you can leave out the "rinse" part.)

This exercise:
- Helps a speaker pace himself.
- Connects the speaker with listeners.
- Forces a speaker to eliminate the non-words ("um," "uh," "like," and "you know.")

Result:
- Speaker fully engages audience.
- Speaker comes across as credible and confident.

ABOUT THE PAUSE

Pauses are critically important to a speaker—and his audience. Each pause gives the speaker time to gather his next thought. It gives the listeners time to reflect on what's just been said.

Note: **When a speaker seems to race on too quickly, it's usually not the rate at which he's speaking that's at fault, it's that he fails to make those vital pauses in his speech.**

Mastery of pause

gives a speaker time to think.

It gives listeners

time to absorb.

The Case against Non-words

The Big Four non-words are: "Um," "uh," "like," and "you know." Two other common non-words are "so" and "and."

Non-words siphon off power from your presentation. Sprinkle too many of them in a speech, and audience members begin to think, "Why is he wasting my time?"

Audiences want to listen to speakers who sound authoritative. Too many non-words erode your authority.

The key thing to realize is: **Almost all speakers who use non-words drop them in *between* thoughts—specifically between sentences or clauses (key parts of sentences).**

Train yourself to *pause* between thoughts. Take the time to pause, and you will find you automatically stop saying the non-words.

The next step in leadership communications mastery extends your reach. Now you will take your mastery of Focus and build on it by applying it in a "real world" exercise.

Here goes:

Step Two:

Advanced Focus—

The Three Kinds of Sentences

& Real-world Communication

Now we're ready to go from the ball park to the boardroom. The next exercise covers the three kinds of sentences used in real-world communication. It applies what you've mastered in the 7th Inning Stretch exercise to real-world business communications.

First, locate a speech text or a presentation you have delivered, or plan to deliver. If you prefer, you can use the excerpt from the text of President Ronald Reagan's Challenger Disaster Speech (page 68). It will work for this exercise.

Whether you use your own material, or the Reagan speech, you'll find real-world speeches will contain sentences more complex than the sentences of "Take Me Out to the Ball Game."

The eight sentences in "Take Me Out to the Ball Game" are all short simple sentences. Speeches and presentations you deliver in the "real world" will contain simple sentences, but also will contain longer and more complex sentences.

Most business communications contain three kinds of sentences:

- *Simple*—sentences with a subject, verb and object.

- *Compound*—two simple sentences linked together by "and," "but," or some other conjunction.

- *Complex*—a simple or compound sentence containing subjects, verbs and/or objects with simple or complex modifiers (adverbs, adjectives, or clauses).

Most speeches and presentations are made up of a mlx of the above types of sentences.

In Step Two practice sessions, you will deliver your "real world" text, using the skills you've mastered in the **Focus** exercise. But this time, you don't necessarily pause only at the end of a sentence. Instead, working with more complex sentences, you will pause when you complete either a sentence—or a phrase—or a clause.

Newbies to Step Two often feel the skills required to deliver a speech from a more complex speech text will be difficult to master. With practice, they realize that transferring what they've learned in Step One to Step Two is very do-able.

Vautier's Words to the Wise

Next time you plan to give a speech from a prepared text:

- *Use a larger font (easier to see)*
- *Break the text into "easy for the eye to capture" bracketed segments. We recommend two columns per page.*

You read the columns top down. Each bracketed segment equals the "one thought" the speaker needs to gather and then deliver to one set of eyes. (Many professional speechwriters prepare texts for their executive speakers this way.)

See the excerpt from Ronald Reagan's Challenger speech (next page). It has been formatted this way. Segments can be enclosed in brackets with either a pen (as shown), or with a word processor.

Speech text formatted for presentation:

Ronald Reagan's Speech
following the Challenger Disaster

. . . We've grown used to wonders in this century.

There will be more shuttle flights and more shuttle crews

It's hard to dazzle us. But for twenty-five years the United States space program has been doing just that.

and, yes, more volunteers, more civilians, more teachers in space. Nothing ends here;

We've grown used to the idea of space,

our hopes and our journeys continue.

and, perhaps we forget that we've only just begun.

I want to add that I wish I could talk to every man and woman who works for NASA, or who worked on this mission

We're still pioneers. They, the members of the Challenger crew, were pioneers. . . .

We'll continue our quest in space.

and tell them: "Your dedication and professionalism have moved and impressed us for decades.

And we know of your anguish. We share it."

There's a coincidence today.

On this day three hundred and ninety years ago,

the great explorer Sir Francis Drake died aboard ship off the coast of Panama.

In his lifetime the great frontiers were the oceans,

and a historian later said, "He lived by the sea, died on it, and was buried in it."

Well, today, we can say of the Challenger crew:

Their dedication was, like Drake's, complete.

The crew of the space shuttle Challenger honored us

by the manner in which they lived their lives.

We will never forget them, nor the last time we saw them,

this morning, as they prepared for their journey and waved goodbye and "slipped the surly bonds of earth" to "touch the face of God."

WORK OUTSIDE 'THE BOX'

When you speak or present, seated: Imagine an invisible box that starts south of your chin and north of the table, and that extends to the outside edges of your shoulders.

In Europe and America, by longstanding tradition, when you are seated at a table, this "box" is your personal space. You own it for the length of time you are seated at that table. By the same token, the people seated to your left and right "own" the personal spaces in their "boxes." For seated presentations, you gesture within the box. If you gesture so widely that you intrude on your neighbors' personal spaces, your body language says "thoughtless" and even "aggressive." (Note: You also want to avoid clasping your hands together when seated. Open hands are a universal symbol of trust, generosity, and receptivity.) However, when you deliver a speech standing, in front of a room, you gesture above the waist, and *outside* the box.

DO THIS:

Stand balanced 50-50, on both feet. Arms at sides, hands open. Gesture outside the torso, hands open.

DON'T DO THIS:

Fig leaf position   **Arms folded**   **Weight unevenly**

(defensive)   (defensive)   distributed

Why You Should Avoid The 'Fig Leaf position': or, the Do's and Don'ts of Executive Presence

Are there specific things a speaker or presenter should and should not do to convey executive presence when speaking or presenting?

Yes. The following do's and don'ts and recommendations provide the specific how-to's of communicating executive presence in a speech or presentation.

Do this & don't do that

when you speak

standing in front of a room

(See next pages.)

HANDS / GESTURES

- *Do* **use your hands to gesture**. Hand gestures are effective at keeping your audience's attention.

- *Do* **gesture outside your body.** As you gesture, your elbows should not be locked to your waist (the Velcro effect). There should be air between your arms and your torso. Gesture outside the lines created from the outside of your shoulders to the floor. The "arms held away from the body" pose visually opens up your body, and automatically makes you more expressive. You come across looking more comfortable and more engaging.

- *Do* **gesture with your hands** *up above your waist.* The eye travels to flashes of light, color, and motion. If you are speaking without slides, you won't create light or color as you speak or present. You are limited to motion, and you create motion with your hand gestures.

- *Don't* **gesture below the waist.** When you're standing in front of a room, without a lectern, if you make gestures below your waist, at hip level, your audiences eyes will travel to your hands. You want their attention focused on your upper torso.

- *Don't* **close your hands.** This means don't curl them into fists at your sides. Don't cup them. (Remember, a hand offered in a handshake is fully open. The open hand is a universal symbol of trust and teamwork. An open hand is more expressive and makes you look more approachable.)

- ***Don't* bring your hands together in the "Fig Leaf position"** (hands clasped together over your lower torso). This is universal defensive body language—the opposite of open and confident body language. For the same reason, don't clasp your hands behind your back.

EXECUTIVE STANCE
Neutral Position

Neutral Position, Standing Behind a Lectern:

Rest your hands (open) on top of the lectern. Use your hands to gesture above the lectern (again open). When you gesture *above* the lectern your Executive Presence increases.

Don't "grab the rails" of the lectern. When you "grab the rails," the only hand gestures you can make are small hand movements—usually just your fingers flexing from the rail.

Neutral Position, Standing 'Front and Center':

Neutral position when you stand in front of an audience without a lectern is when you stand with your (open) hands draped down to your sides. When you gesture, you raise your hands above the waist, outside the body lines (or, outside "the Box"—the rectangle created by your torso) with your hands open.

Leaving the "core" of your body "open" helps you look more approachable. This is because if you bring your hands to rest *inside* your body lines (i.e., in front of your torso), or if you gesture inside your body lines, you create a visual barrier between yourself and the audience.

The Neutral Positions are among the most difficult physical presence skills to learn, so you need to consciously master them. This is because, for most of us, our "muscle memory" (where our hands go to rest when we're not thinking about it) is generally "inside the Box."

Again, the Neutral Positions increase your Executive Presence. You may not *feel* it, but to observers, you will *look* more comfortable, confident and at ease.

MOVEMENT

- *Do* **maintain visual balance in the way you move and stand.** If you start to take a step forward or to the side, finish the step. Coming to rest in a half-step stance results in visual imbalance.

- *Don't* **move constantly.** Don't rock back and forth, or right and left as you speak.

- *Don't* **stand motionless in one spot throughout your speech or presentation.** Use hand gestures. Or, get out from behind the lectern and move toward an audience member now and then. (This may need to wait until you are more advanced—and a bit more confident—as a speaker.)

- ***Do* walk in the direction you are looking and talking when you move** (i.e., make eye contact with someone in the direction of the room where you want to go, and move in that direction. When you arrive at your destination—a step or two away—stop and rebalance yourself. Your feet should end up side by side).

> **A person who is visually balanced appears strong, confident, and in command—leadership qualities you want to project.**
>
> **For this reason, avoid gestures and movements that destroy visual balance—resting your weight on one leg, placing a hand on a hip, etc.**

EYES

- ***Do* practice Focus.** Deliver one complete thought to one pair of eyes.

- ***Do* glance down at your notes, as needed, as you pause. Find your thought and gather it.** Then look up at a set of eyes. Speak the complete thought to that person.

- ***Don't* talk to a laptop or a sheet of paper** (i.e., with your eyes glued to your notes, speech text, index cards, PowerPoint screen, etc.)

- ***Don't* scan the room** (i.e., don't look at multiple pairs of eyes while delivering a single thought).

VOICE

- ***Do* use your one-to-group voice** (your voice at a 7-to-8 level—your "speaker's voice").

- ***Don't* use your one-to-one voice** (i.e., don't use your voice at a low 3-to-4 level—the voice you use at the breakfast table, or in the coffee break room).

- ***Do* use your one-to-group inflection** (a more emphatic version of your one-to-one inflection in which you stress important words, phrases or sentences.

- ***Don't* use your one-to-one inflection**. It will be too bland in a group.

- ***Do* control the pace of your speech** by using **Focus,** the eye contact method. (See the section on **Focus** earlier in this chapter.)

- **_Do_ pause when you finish delivering one thought** (one sentence or clause).
- **_Do_ keep non-words at bay** (also using the eye contact method).

Do this & don't do that
when you speak
from a seated position:

When you present from a seated position, the only thing listeners see moving are your hands above the table—within "the box" (created by the space below your chin, above the table, and within the outside edges of your shoulders). When not moving, your hands should come to rest, open—not closed, on top of the table. This is the Executive Presence neutral position when seated. (When standing, you gesture outside of the box. Seated, you gesture inside the box. Seated, your gestures are literally more contained.)

Here are the do's and don'ts for speaking from a seated position:

HANDS

- **_Do_ rest your hands, up to your wrists, either palms down or on the outside edge of your pinkies** on the table, on either side of your notes or laptop.

Your hands remain open, as mentioned above. This is the neutral position.

GESTURES

- *Do* **occasionally gesture in the direction of an audience member** with whom you have made eye contact.

- *Do* **imagine an invisible box around yourself** that starts south of your chin and north of the table, and extends to the outside of your shoulders. Limit your hand gestures to the space within this box.

- *Do* **return your hands to neutral position (hands on top of the table) when you are not using them to gesture.**

- *Don't* **put your forearms on the table.** Here's why: When you gesture, if your forearms are on the table, your hands can move only in a very limited way, as if invisible Velcro keeps your arms glued to the table. The other reason to avoid placing the forearms on the table is that, once you do that, you tend to hunch your shoulders. Your whole body takes on a less open, more closed-in look.

- ***Don't* close your hands, or half close them, or clasp them together.** You may allow your hands to curve slightly, but keep them open. (When you're seated at a table in a meeting room, the open hand is even more important as less of you is visible. That means that what is visible telegraphs your body language to your listeners even more powerfully.)

POSTURE

- ***Do* sit up in your chair.** (Mom was right.) Don't lean back against the chair. Buttocks should be against the back of the chair. Upper back should be about three inches away from the upper back of the chair (about a fist distant).
- ***Do* position your legs appropriately. Women cross legs. Men place feet flat on the floor.**

VOICE / EYES

Same as when standing.

ADDITIONAL

- If you have distributed handouts, as is often the case with seated presentations, you might direct your listeners' attention to specific points on the handout.

A Shout Out for Volume

One key characteristic of a speaker's voice is that it is *loud*.

It *projects*.

If you assign a numerical value to volume, with 1 being the lowest (a whisper), and 10 the highest (a shout), the ordinary speaking voice you use at the breakfast table or in the coffee break room would range from 3-to-4 in volume. We call this your one-to-one Volume. Your speaker's voice should be at a 7-to-8 volume level.

But won't I be too loud?

Most people fear that if they raise their voices to "speaker's voice" level, they will come across as aggressively and obnoxiously loud.

Trust us: 95% of all speakers are *not loud enough*. If we were with you and able to whisper in your ear as you delivered any given speech or presentation, we would undoubtedly be whispering two words to you: "Louder. Louder."

Why is this? Most of us tend to speak too softly because without training and awareness, it's natural for us to calibrate our voices to our one-to-one vocal level.

But we need to amp up our volume when we speak to a group. If we don't, we will fail to grab our audience's attention. The problem is, we need to get used to speaking at the higher volume. At first, it sounds awkward to us.

What newbie speakers don't realize is that their speaker's voice does *not* sound awkward to the audiences they address. In group coaching sessions, we see it happen again and again: If you ask audience members, "Is Bob/Jill too loud?" you'll hear a chorus of "No's."

So you need to consciously work to calibrate your speaker's voice to the one-to-group level—your speaker's voice level—when you give a speech or presentation.

Initially, because it's something you're not accustomed to, it may feel overdone and not natural to you.

But it won't be.

When is a speaker "over the top"?

As mentioned in Chapter 2, a video that went viral on YouTube.com features Microsoft chairman Steve Ballmer starting a speech by shouting at the audience at the top of his lungs. The video provides an example of over the top.

(Enter the search words "Steve Ballmer" on YouTube.com to view the video.)

Ballmer goes too far.

But will you do that? No. Again, almost all speakers *don't go far enough.*

Feel comfortable

when you begin to use

your speaker's voice?

Then you are not loud enough.

After you get used to delivering speeches and presentations with your speaker's voice, you will discover that your comfort level with a higher volume will increase.

THE 3 LEVELS OF ENGAGEMENT

As a speaker, you need to know that there are three levels of engagement:

Level 1: Speaker makes eye contact with an audience member for a full thought. In our coaching sessions, we call this **Focus**. (Eyes)

Level 2: Speaker makes eye contact and gestures toward that audience member. (Eyes / Hands)

Level 3: Speaker makes eye contact, gestures toward, and takes a step toward that audience member. (Eyes / Hands / Body)

What happens when you are in the audience and the speaker makes eye contact with you, gestures toward you, and walks toward you as he does so? You become more alert, don't you? In fact, you are riveted. So are the other audience members. You also tend to view the speaker as confidently taking command of the room. That's engagement. The speaker now has your full attention.

Engagement begins with the eyes, and the eyes control it. Gestures and bodily movement reinforce eye contact. But the eyes remain key at each of the three levels of engagement.

5 - When *You're* the Message

Make the Message Count

- The 7 Factors That Determine Executive Presence
- So How *Does* a Speaker Model Executive Presence?
- Pacesetter Presidential Communicators: Kennedy to Obama
- What Today's Speakers Can Learn from the Greats of the Past

Roger Ailes, chairman of Fox Television Stations Group and media consultant for Presidents Richard Nixon, Ronald Reagan, and George H. W. Bush, wrote a book titled *You Are the Message*.

He makes the point that when we communicate to others, it's not just with words.

Ailes is exactly right. People don't just *listen* to us. They take in the volume, tone and pitch of our voices; our facial expressions; our eye contact (or lack thereof), and our body language (how we hold ourselves and how we move).

People also sense our level of sincerity—our passion and commitment to the messages we broadcast—not to mention how we make them feel. They note whether we make them tense up, or bore them, or grasp their interest, or make them laugh and smile.

They look to see if our words are in sync with everything else we project to them.

An example: If an army recruiter gets up to speak to a group of young men and women about the benefits of a career in the military, but his uniform is stained and wrinkled, he appears bored or arrogant or hung over, and he's rude and dismissive to his audience and clearly wishes he were someplace else, it doesn't matter how well written his speech may be. His physical presence will undercut his message. To paraphrase Roger Ailes, "*He* becomes the message." In this case, the message is not positive.

The disheveled army recruiter in our example needs to do a better job of projecting "military presence" when he speaks—not to mention adjusting his attitude.

As a professional on the leadership track, you need to be mindful of projecting "executive presence" when you speak. Fortunately, the skill of projecting executive presence can be learned.

The 7 Factors

That Determine

Executive Presence

Let's recap what determines Executive Presence: In addition to the face you were born with (which is not under your control), and the apparel you buy and your grooming (which *are* under your control), there are seven elements of executive presence that particularly relate to public speaking.

- Three are **VISUAL** (the way you look):
    - eyes
    - hands
    - posture

- Four are **AURAL** (the way you sound):
    - volume
    - inflection
    - pace
    - non-words

> If you lack confidence in your clothing choices, enlist the aid of a professional stylist, or of savvy salespeople at upscale department stores. Explain the dress code in your place of business, and that you've been advised to dress like "executive material." Both stylists and sales professionals can make excellent and knowledgeable suggestions.

Governor Chris Christie Rocks Executive Presence

Chris Christie (who took office as Governor of New Jersey in 2010) exudes executive presence. Certainly he dresses to fit a leadership role. But clothes are only a part of it. Sure, if he wore a poorly cut, wrinkled suit, it would detract from his leadership look. But, take the suit away, and Governor Christie still projects leadership style. This was evident after the 2012 Hurricane Sandy disaster. He appeared on television news programs in casual clothing, with wind tunnel hair. But his distracted appearance did not detract from his executive presence. In fact, his TV appearances during the disaster emphasized how Christie's executive presence stems from the way he carries himself, his eye contact, his posture, and the way he speaks.

You've heard the joke, "He has a face made for radio"? That one-liner grew out of the fact that more than one successful radio personality has a voice that *projects* executive presence. When you meet the speaker, however, you see an unimpressive figure, and think, "You've gotta be kidding me."

Radio personalities grow their audiences because, on radio, only the quality of the *voice* matters. The rest of us need to pay attention to additional factors.

So How *Does* a Speaker Model Executive Presence?

It's a "show me" world. So how does a speaker or presenter "show" executive presence?

On the next page (in the left hand column) are the aspects of public speaking a speaker can work at and finesse. The right hand column shows the attributes accrued.

Focus	Confident
Gestures	Credible
Movement	Compelling
Volume	Professional
Inflection	Genuine
Momentum	Interesting
Non-words	Natural (minimal)

This book outlines the steps you need to take to achieve maximum executive presence in each of these areas.

In addition to the face you were born with (which is not under your control), and the apparel you buy and your grooming (which *are* under your control), there are seven elements of executive presence that particularly relate to public speaking: eyes, hands, posture, volume, inflect-tion, pace, and controlling "non-words."

JOHN M. VAUTIER & JOHN J. VAUTIER

Pacesetter Presidential Communicators: Kennedy to Obama

When our nation's chief executive is able to set a new standard in communication, that standard trickles down into the business world. Presidents can set the pace.

Since the 1960s, which Presidential communicators stand on the pinnacle? Four come to mind: John F. Kennedy, Ronald Reagan, Bill Clinton, and Barack Obama. They are important to all speakers and presenters today. Why? Because these very capable Presidential role models shaped the standards for modern executive communications.

Kennedy began the era of the modern executive communicator. If delivered today, the language of his speeches—penned by gifted speechwriter Ted Sorensen—would seem too formal. But Kennedy brought something new to the speaker's platform—youthful exuberance and energy. A passionate presence, Kennedy moved audiences, even lifted them up. He connected with listeners and viewers in a way his predecessors and contemporaries could rarely match. That style (Kennedy's style)—direct, energetic, sometimes breezy—is where expectations for today's executive communicators began to take shape.

Presidents Lyndon Johnson, Richard Nixon, Jimmy Carter and Gerald Ford followed. They were "workmanlike" speakers—they delivered their messages to a certain standard. But they failed to connect deeply with audiences.

Then came three more superstar Presidential communicators— Ronald Reagan, Bill Clinton, and—shortly afterwards—Barack Obama. Each of these Presidents represents a giant spike in leadership communication excellence. They connected and connect

90

with audiences ably and often movingly. Kennedy, Reagan, Clinton, and Obama—since 1960, those are the four high points.

What has changed since Kennedy's day? The key change is that speakers have traveled a continuum away from **speeching** and toward **speaking**—from the "high style" (the lofty and formal rhetoric) of Kennedy's speeches to today's informality, with speeches that are often delivered in language so casual it comes across as conversational in tone.

What today's speakers can learn from the greats of the past

It is interesting to look at the "backdrop" behind each of the four outstanding Presidential speakers—at who was around them at the time, or at who had preceded them. Each of the four great communicator Presidents benefited by finding a way to meet the needs of their times, but also by contrasting with blander competitors or predecessors who had failed to fully connect with their audiences. The Four Greats each filled a void a majority of the public was hungry to have filled.

When Kennedy emerged on the national scene, the United States was leaving the '50's behind, and entering the turbulent '60's. The world began to change dramatically. The youth culture emerged. Kennedy's youth and passion fit the times.

Kennedy also was a refreshing new face following the Presidency of grandfatherly Dwight Eisenhower and his Vice President, straitlaced and lawyerly Richard Nixon. Reagan, despite his advanced years, provided a vigorous image compared to bland Jimmy Carter.

In addition, when Reagan ran against Carter, the backdrop was a weak and struggling America, and a seemingly less than approachable

President. The nation welcomed Reagan's "yes, we can" optimism, his defiant stance against Communism, and his approachability.

Bill Clinton "felt our pain" while his predecessor George Bush stood out in our minds for disliking broccoli, and Senator Bob Dole, the candidate Clinton ran against, seemed cold, stiff and formal at the podium. Barack Obama promised "change we could believe in" against the backdrop of a crumbling economy, and campaigned against Senator John McCain, who struggled to ignite excitement in his audiences.

Because their predecessors provided such stark contrasts, the Four Greats were better received by the public than they might otherwise have been.

Senator Bob Dole, by the way, was very likable to people who knew him well, but failed to consistently project that amiability as a speaker. During his run for the Presidency, there were occasions when he appeared mellow and approachable. At other times he appeared gruff and irritated. As a professional speech coach, I find it baffling that Senator Dole didn't take the time to locate and work with a coach who could have helped him to consistently bring out that amiable side of him during the race for the Presidency.

Interestingly, Senator Dole had no trouble projecting that likability in the commercials he later did for American Express. Clearly he had a director and received coaching for the commercials. But, just as clearly, it appears that the ability to project that amiable quality was quite do-able for him as a candidate—yet he failed to exercise it in a way that might have made a difference.

One hallmark of the four Presidents who set communication standards for us over the last several decades is the consistency of the public persona they project.

Whether making a formal presentation, giving a media interview, or chatting informally while interacting with constituents, they all appear down-to-earth and approachable, no matter what situation they are in. They all are able to reach out and connect with people.

Genuineness and likability are expected elements of executive presence in today's world. Today, a distant autocratic style won't work in politics, and it doesn't fly in business. The formal, reclusive persona will not be the leader of the future.

6 - Stand and Deliver

- **Message Organization**
- **Build It Back to Front (Not Front to Back)**
- **Bold Beginnings/Masterful Middles (Forms of Influence-SPEAK)/How to End**
- **How to Make Your Speech "Sticky" (& Why You Should)**
- **How to Begin—Bob Dole's Most Memorable Speech**
- **Looks matter: your presentation options (PowerPoint, KeyNote & Prezi)**

"Begin with the End in Mind."

—*Stephen Covey,* The 7 Habits of Highly Effective People

Alice: *"Would you tell me, please, which way I ought to go from here?"*
Cheshire Cat: *"That depends a good deal on where you want to get to."*
(Often paraphrased as: "If you don't know where you're going, any road will take you there.")

— *Lewis Carroll,* Alice's Adventures in Wonderland

It is not enough to master the skills required to speak effectively in front of an audience. You also need to prepare (or have someone prepare) a speech or presentation that presents good, well-organized information.

'Flight Plan' for a Speech

1. Tell them what you're going to tell them

2. Deliver:

- **Argument 1**

- **Argument 2**

- **Argument 3**

3. Tell them what you've told them.

The above "flight plan" for a speech can be expanded with quotations, anecdotes, facts and figures, etc. But the simple framework above provides the basic flow and rhythm of most speeches.

Message

Organization

What is the best way to organize the messages you plan to deliver?

Think about how pilots operate.

Every day, in the United States alone, pilots fly 87,000 aircraft. The skies are filled with everything from commercial airlines to private planes, to military flights. And every pilot is required to file a flight plan. They then fly that flight plan. The only time they ever deviate from the planned course is in the event of a life-threatening emergency.

The system works.

With very rare exceptions, all the many flights that take place across the U.S. take off and land exactly as planned.

Speakers can benefit from a "flight plan" strategy.

How? Simple. Develop a "plan" (a system of organization) for your content. And stick to your plan. Most speeches and presentations can be built on a simple pattern you can easily memorize, and then adapt to any situation. Take the time to internalize the plan. You will have the confidence of knowing you can tap into that format to effectively deliver any messages you are called upon to deliver.

Build it Back to Front

(Not Front to Back)

What is the most important advice we can give you about preparing a speech or a presentation?
Here it is: **In putting your remarks together, start with the end in mind.** In other words, before you do anything else: *determine what you will say in your final sentence or two* (when you sum up your key messages). Why? Because deciding this ensures a clear direction for your speech. It enables you to organize your thoughts effectively.

When you know your destination,

you'll know where you're going,

& how to map out your way there.

The most common mistake made in writing a speech is that the speech is thought through "front to back"—i.e., from the beginning to the end.

People fire up PowerPoint, then ask themselves, "Now, what do I want to say?" Then they start creating: slide 1, slide 2, and so on.

One serious problem you encounter when you build this way (from the front forward), is that it's easy to get off the right path and digress. You don't have a "True North" end point in mind. That means you are more likely to wander in several directions.

So, when you begin to construct a speech, ask yourself: "When I'm done speaking, what do I want listeners to *do*, to *know*, and/or to *believe*?" The answer to this question is your "thesis."

Then ask yourself: what three arguments can I make to take my listeners with me, logically, and have them arrive at the place I need them to arrive? (There may be more than three or four arguments. If so, pick the three or four most compelling.)

Using this approach, you then construct your speech—every element you add as you construct your speech should support your end goal, your thesis.

This technique is called building a speech from "back to front."

The middle of your speech—composed of the three logical arguments you use to support your thesis—will fall into place naturally—if you know the conclusion you aim to achieve.

The THESIS of your speech =

what you want listeners

TO DO, TO KNOW,

and/or TO BELIEVE

when you stop talking.

> **Writing a speech?**
>
> **Figure out your ending.**
>
> **Then craft your opening remarks.**
>
> **After that, fill in the middle—**
>
> **but *always***
>
> **start with the end in mind.**

Your Bold Beginning

Once you know the conclusion you want to reach, the next step is easy. You create your introduction. Introduce your speech with a bold interesting statement.

You may choose to share a startling fact or statistic in your opening lines. You may begin with a killer quote. You may share an analogy.

Whatever you choose to do to begin your talk, your opening remarks should be attention grabbing. They should make your audience eager to hear your supporting arguments.

End result: Know This, Do This, Believe This

Vautier's Words to the Wise: Go to the Source

It's often a good idea to call whoever issued the invitation to speak, and ask, "What does the audience want to hear?" You might be surprised. This kind of inquiry often yields insights that enable you to prepare remarks that best suit your listeners' interests—and to tailor your presentation to meet your objectives.

Masterful Middles

Once you have your audience's attention, your next step is to present those three compelling arguments that make your case. You may know your material cold. Or you may need to do some research and make some calls. But once you have collected the material that supports your key arguments, you will find you have a collection of what are called Forms of Influence (FOIs).

There are six major Forms of Influence. They are easy to remember if you use the acronym **SPEAK**.

SPEAK stands for: **statistics and facts, personal experience, examples, analogies, and the killer quote (or the quotable sound bite).**

FOI

(FORMS OF INFLUENCE)

Statistics & Facts

Personal experience

Examples

Analogies

Killer quotes &

Following are some examples of FOIs excerpted from a few recent standout speeches.

FOI—persuasive statistics and facts

In the example that follows, Randy Larsen, Colonel, USAF (Ret.) and national security adviser, uses compelling statistics and facts to bring home various points in a speech that advocates common sense and resourceful thinking in dealing with terrorist threats. Throughout his speech, he draws an analogy to a medical pioneer's successful "war" on smallpox.

Excerpts from speech follow:

> According to the WHO, one billion people were afflicted with smallpox in the 20th century. Three hundred million died. Most of the survivors were horribly scarred, and many were left blind. Three hundred million—that is a difficult figure to comprehend. To better put this in perspective, a study by the New York Times stated that the total death toll from warfare in the 20th century—from both direct and indirect causes—was one hundred million.

The above statistic provides a perspective for the importance of the victory over smallpox. Later in his speech, Colonel Larsen notes the illogic of scanning shipping containers for terrorist weapons, using facts and statistics to make his case:

> . . . For instance, last summer Congress passed legislation requiring 100% radiological scanning of shipping containers entering the United States. Just like those who called for mass vaccination, 100% percent scanning is not the answer to the problem. The reason Congress called for 100% radiological scanning is because they asked the wrong question. They asked, "what do we do to prevent al Qaeda, or any other terrorist organization, from smuggling a nuclear weapon into the United States?"

> That's the wrong question. Do we really believe that if a terrorist organization got their hands on one or two nuclear weapons they would actually put them in a shipping container,

put a real good padlock on the door, and then turn it loose into a global transportation system—a system in which numerous different companies would at one time or another touch that container en route to the United States? I don't think they are that stupid. Neither does the chief of security at the Port Authority of New York and New Jersey, Beth Anne Rooney. She talks about how foolish it is to scan 100% of the shipping containers coming into the port, but do nothing about the 880,000 cars that come into the port every year on roll-on roll-off ships, and drive out of the port without any scanning whatsoever. The critical components of a Hiroshima-sized nuke can easily fit into a small car.

Colonel Larsen compares the budget allocated to collecting loose nuclear material to that allocated for "two to three days in Iraq" to make the point that "asking the wrong questions" can lead to the wrong prioritization of action items:

. . . Initiatives such as the Nunn-Lugar Cooperative Threat Reduction program can provide far better returns on investment than 100% scanning. However, today we spend only about one billion dollars a year on Nunn-Lugar-type programs to prevent terrorist organizations from becoming nuclear powers. That is what we spend every two to three days in Iraq. And according to the report from the bi-partisan Robb-Silberman Commission, "The United States has not made intelligence collection on loose nuclear material a high priority."

Can anyone here tell me what might be a higher priority?

LESSONS LEARNED FROM "A GOOD WAR"
Address by RANDALL J. LARSEN, USAF (Ret.) Colonel &
National Security Advisor, Center for Biosecurity,
University of Pittsburgh Medical Center

FOI—personal experience and analogy

Actor Erik Stolhanske, the speaker in the next example, has effectively dealt with a lifelong physical challenge. He uses **personal experience** *to draw an effective* **analogy** *in the conclusion of his speech which is a call to "believe this," "know this," and "do this."*

Excerpt from speech follows:

> I was born without a fibula in my right leg. It was just one of those genetic mistakes.
>
> Now, 30 years later, I can lift up the hem of my pants and show people my prosthetic leg, and when I see their jaws drop, I'm totally fine with it. But when I was 8, I wanted to die when I heard names like "Gimp," "Woody," and "Cripple"—and that's just what my sister called me!...

Conclusion of speech:

> And, although you may not have prosthetic body parts, everyone has a "wooden leg" of some kind. I'm living proof that once you realize that your "wooden leg," whatever it may be, is really just in your head, that's when you can stay true to yourself, pursue your dreams with foolish perseverance, and truly achieve success in life—whatever that may mean to you.
>
> *"BE A LITTLE DELUSIONAL"*
> *Address by ERIK STOLHANSKE, Writer and Actor*
> *Delivered at the Fox '59 Leadership Institute,*
> *Colgate University, Hamilton, N.Y., April 3, 2012*

FOI—quotable sound bite

Broadcasting executive Roger Ailes claims to have given Reagan the lines, "I want you to know that also I will not make age an issue of this campaign. I am not going to exploit for political purposes my opponent's youth and inexperience."

That remark effectively pushed back on the criticism that Reagan was too old to run for the Presidency and helped decide the election in Reagan's favor.

Powerful language is language that makes a point with humor, poignancy, or passion. It sparks emotions in listeners. Important messages penetrate minds and hearts on those waves of emotion.

> # Keep them glued:
>
> # quotes, anecdotes,
>
> # analogies, & acronyms
>
> # liven presentations.

FOI—personal experience

and quotable sound bite

TED is a nonprofit organization that hosts conferences featuring "the world's most fascinating thinkers and doers [giving] the talk of their lives (in 18 minutes or less)." Many of these speeches (the "TED Talks") are posted online.

In one TED conference, Mark Bezos, who heads up development for a charitable organization in New York City, and who is assistant captain of a volunteer fire company in New York, related the story of how he showed up at his first fire. He raced to the captain to find out what his assignment would be. The captain was speaking to the home-owner who was standing under an umbrella in the pouring rain, barefoot in her pajamas.

Bezos had been harboring the hope he would be assigned to save a life but found that all the people in the building had safely exited. The captain asked Bezos to go into the home and bring the homeowner a pair of shoes.

Bezos entered the building, found the homeowner a pair of shoes, and brought them out to her. He felt the action was insignificant. However, he says, a few weeks later, the woman wrote to the fire department thanking all who had made such valiant efforts to save her home. "The act of kindness she remembered above all others?" Bezos asked his audience. "Someone had even brought her a pair of shoes."

Bezos summed up the point of his story: "I have witnessed acts of generosity and kindness on a monumental scale but I've also witnessed acts of grace and courage on an individual basis and you know what I've learned? They all matter."

In concluding, he urged audience members not to put off their generosity. "If you have something to give, give it now . . . . Not every day offers us an opportunity to save a life. But every day offers us the opportunity to affect one. So get in the game. *Save the shoes.*"

(To view Mark Bezos's speech, "A life lesson from a volunteer firefighter," visit Ted.com and enter "Mark Bezos" in the site's search box.)

FOI—acronym

In his speeches, motivational lecturer Tony Robbins uses the acronym FEAR to make a point about the importance of not overestimating the obstacles and challenges each of us face. FEAR, he tells his audiences, is an acronym that stands for "False Evidence Appearing Real."

NASA scientist Jonathan Trent, who is advancing a plan to grow new biofuel by farming micro-algae, gave a speech to the TED organization about his work. He calls the system OMEGA, an acronym for Offshore Membrane Enclosures for Growing Algae. "At NASA, you have to have good acronyms," he quips.

Killer Quotations

Several online sites provide collections of quotations you can search by keyword or subject matter, including:
- **GoodReads**--http://www.goodreads.com/quotes
- **Great-Quotes**—Great-Quotes.com
- **The Quote Garden**—http://www.quotegarden.com/
- **Quotations Page**—http://www.quotationspage.com/
- **BrainyQuote**—http://www.brainyquote.com/

Keep your message simple

& on track

If someone asked you, "Want to hear a really long story?" how would you react?

Most people would turn down the offer.

Audiences' attention spans have grown shorter in the last few decades. Hollywood knows this. It's the rare movie that lasts longer than 90 minutes— despite the fact that movies have an arsenal of lures to hold audiences, including A-list actors, top-notch screenwriting, award-winning musical scores, and whiz-bang special effects.

Despite all those ways of making a movie as alluring as possible, Hollywood moviemakers know they shouldn't push a too-long movie on audiences. Every bit of dialogue, scenery, or action needs to earn its place in the movie. It needs to add in some way to the story.

Why, then, do speakers think they can hold an audience's attention when they ramble in their speeches? They can't.

Good speakers avoid pointless digressions.

Story Discipline

The BAR

The stories and anecdotes used to illustrate your speech can range from personal experiences to scientific case studies.

First, make sure the story or anecdote you are about to share works to support or illustrate a point you wish to make in your speech. The point of the story should tie in to the end result you are aiming to achieve.

You also need to tell your story economically for it to be most effective. That means avoid digressions. Here's a great formula you can use to ensure just that. It's called the BAR formula. BAR is short for Background/Action/Result.

The BAR formula works this way:

The B A R method provides a universal formula for telling a story in economical prose, as shown on the page that follows.

Background—provide the background to the story you are telling.

Action—explain the action the background situation sparked.

Results—share the results of the action.

Following are some examples of BARs:

*The following **BAR** anecdote details how action taken by **Ford Motor Company's CFO** helped Ford avert a financial catastrophe.*

- **Background:** Prior to the 2008 economic meltdown, Ford's CFO saw the storm clouds of a deep recession approach.
- **Action:** To prepare Ford to weather the storm, the CFO mortgaged a good portion of Ford's assets including the Mustang brand, the Ford logo, and even the company's famous Glass House headquarters building.
- **Result:** Ford was prepared with a seven-billion-dollar cash reserve when the severe recession of 2008 hit. Ford weathered the recession without needing a government bailout, and emerged healthy and standing on its own two feet.

*The following **BAR** anecdote, used in a speech that Mary Sue Coleman—President of the University of*

Michigan—delivered to a group of student winners of a science talent search contest, points out that scientific discoveries have no "shelf date."

- **Background:** Sixty years ago, University of Michigan graduate Dr. Jerome Horwitz sought to find a drug that would treat cancer.

- **Action:** Dr. Horwitz conducted research and, in 1964, after several years, created a compound he believed would be effective in slowing the growth of cancer cells. However, tests on mice proved that the drug was not effective. The drug was considered a failure.

- **Result:** Twenty years later, as AIDS began to emerge, another researcher, Dr. Samuel Broder at the National Cancer Institute, sought desperately for something to stop AIDS. Dr. Broder tested Dr. Horwitz's almost forgotten compound and found that it had the effect of transforming AIDS from a death sentence to a chronic disease. The drug was AZT.

The BAR anecdote below was delivered in a speech given by Netherlands Chief of Defense General Peter Van Uhm. The speaker makes the point that a gun can be a powerful instrument of peace.

- **Background:** General Van Uhm relates a story his father told him. During World War Two, when the Nazis invaded the Netherlands, General Van Uhm says his father worked with the resistance.

- **Action:** General Van Uhm's father—a crack shot—positioned himself across the river from the Nazi soldiers invading his country. The general's father fired on the invaders, but to no effect. "My father had been given an old gun that could not reach the opposite river bank." The general recounts how—for the rest of his life—his father remained frustrated about his inability to fend off his nation's invaders.

- **Result:** In high school, the young Peter Van Uhm made a decision to take up the gun—to protect the vulnerable and to defend democracy.

(To view the general's speech, go to Ted.com and enter the search term "Peter Van Uhm.")

The importance

of stories and examples

Stories help speakers connect with their audiences. Audiences love properly told stories. Stories can make audiences laugh, or gasp or cry. They can literally elicit a visceral reaction in listeners.

You can use stories to create vivid mental images that underscore points you seek to make. You also can use stories and examples to buttress facts and statistics with added dimensions. An example that can paint a vivid mental picture for your audience can help you powerfully underscore a point you are trying to make.

Beginnings:

Begin with a BANG!

How do you begin a speech or a presentation? Get your audience's attention in a powerful way right from the start.

Share a relevant headline from the morning paper, a knock-their-socks-off statistic, a moving story, or a killer quote.

Middles:

Toward & Away from

Motivators

Each of the arguments you make in your speech will make a case "toward" or "away from" something.

Just think about how commercials present information. All commercials are done in "toward" and "away from." Commercials argue one or both (usually both) of the following: "If you use this product/service, good things are likely to happen. If you don't, bad things might accrue."

Allstate Insurance's recent commercials clearly provide examples of both "toward" and "away from."

The Allstate "toward" commercial features Dennis Haysbert—an actor who, by the way, is a great model of executive presence. Haysbert's commercials remind viewers of the benefits they receive from Allstate. Typically the "toward" commercials end with one of the two official Allstate slogans: "Are *you* in good hands?" or "That's Allstate's stand."

Allstate's "toward" commercials appeal to viewers who likely have insurance but who may be open to considering a change of provider—if the benefits (the "toward") of the change are presented in an appealing fashion.

Allstate's "away from" commercials feature actor Dean Winters. Winters plays "Mayhem," a recurring character. Mayhem reminds viewers that if you pay too little for your insurance you may not get the best coverage or service. One Mayhem spot features Winters telling the audience, "I'm your son and, as you well know, I can barely focus on one thing at a time." Mayhem proceeds to mow the lawn, while "focusing" on a football game rather than on the job at hand—and the lawn mower kicks up rocks that do hundreds of dollars worth of damage to a home.

The message of "away from" motivators is: Accidents happen. Be prepared by getting insurance. It is meant to speak to a younger demographic, viewers who might need to be reminded that, without sufficient insurance, they will have to pay out of pocket for any accidents that occur.

So how do you know whether to argue "toward" something or "away from" something in your speech?

You need to know the audience, and know the issue. Then you will know which approach (toward/away from) will work best to direct this audience in the direction you want them to go.

In his recent speech on common sense approaches to national security, "Lessons Learned from 'A Good War,' " Randall J. Larsen (Colonel USAF, retired) utilized "toward" arguments to direct his audience to "know" about, "believe" in, and adopt ("do") common sense solutions in the nation's defense.

To make his arguments, Colonel Larsen drew frequent analogies to the "good war" waged by a small army of dedicated men and women who fought to eradicate smallpox globally back in the 1970s. One of the "toward" arguments Colonel Larsen made is that we, as a nation, need to tap into a readily available resource—volunteers—to prepare and deal with disasters—man-made or terrorist. He told the audience that during Hurricane Rita, the use of trained volunteers multiplied law enforcement officials' manpower tenfold during the hurricane evacuation. Colonel Larsen used a colorful phrase to make this concept of tapping into the power of volunteers "stick" in listeners' minds: He called it "posse-ing up."

He also presented a "toward" argument for the proper use of technology in allaying terrorist threats. He again drew an analogy from the war on smallpox. He told the story of how technologically complex smallpox vaccination "guns" often broke down in third world countries. The solution, he explained, was to replace the unreliable high-tech guns with a new technology—a bifurcated (two-pronged) needle. His key point: The new technology was *simpler not more complex* than the technology it replaced. The vaccination fluid hung suspended between the tines of the needle and the needle effectively delivered the vaccine with a few simple jabs. Cost? Five dollars per thousand needles.

In this "toward" argument, Colonel Larsen made clear that throwing money at a problem in the form of high-tech solutions isn't always the best way to solve it, that adopting and promoting resourcefulness and creativity are better options.

How to End

After you've carefully presented your three key arguments and the supporting SPEAKs for each of them, you need to wrap up your remarks—and you need to do so decisively. You've taken care to research, develop and argue your points. Make sure you don't let your speech die an ugly little quiet death at the end!

> **Maintain strong vocal energy as you close your speech. End your remarks effectively. Your last sentence needs to *sound* like your last sentence. Convey that intentionality.**

However you choose to end your speech, draw it to a close in a way that is satisfying for the audience.

Think about gymnasts. At the end of a routine, a good gymnast lands solidly on his feet and motion ceases. There is no shake or wobble in his feet or legs. That's a well-executed *intentional* conclusion of a performance. It's called "sticking the landing." Viewers process this intentionality as confident assurance. A speaker who intentionally ends his speech well "sticks the landing" and shows the same kind of confident assurance.

At the end of your speech, you need to perform the verbal equivalent of a gymnast's "sticking the landing."

Why? Because if you don't end with that sense of intention, you leave the audience hanging, half wondering if you've finished. Your speech loses luster—and you lose a bit of luster as well.

You can end your speech or presentation several ways, including:

- With a call to action
- With a powerful quote
- With a story that has a powerful impact

An example of a powerful ending follows. Here's how the speech opens:

I'd like to tell you a story about a GP, a radiologist, a pathologist and a psychiatrist. Sounds like the first line of a joke, but it isn't. The GP was me. We were having dinner with our children at an open-air opera in Germany. The place was packed. Everyone was having a good time, when the dreaded happened.

Out of the corner of my eye, I saw an elderly man fall headfirst into his plate. The four of us looked at each other. We knew our meal was over and we swung into action.

Each working to type. The psychiatrist tending to the man's wife. The radiologist searching for a defibrillator. The pathologist pounding on the poor man's chest. Me giving mouth-to-mouth.

From the way he keeled over, it was obvious he was dead. But we knew there was still plenty for us to do. We had to comfort his distressed wife. And we had to keep the crowd calm for 30 minutes, till the paramedics arrived.

When it was over, my 15-year-old son turned to me and said: "I want to be able to do that."

"Do what?" I asked him.

"Care for people," he said.

His reply surprised me. Not just because impressing teenage children isn't easy. But because what impressed him wasn't the glory and the drama of our public display of medical skill. No. What impressed him was our simple act of caring. Caring for a sick man. Caring for the man's wife. And caring for the people in the crowd. That's what inspired my son. And that's how my father inspired me a generation ago.

And here's how the speaker concludes her speech:

We need to remind ourselves why we entered this honourable profession in the first place. When I come home from work and my son asks me what sort of day I've had, on a good day I want to be able to say "I saved a life," not "I met a budget." ... I am convinced that there are enough of us to create a revolution in healthcare. Not a revolution that the government is talking about in the bill—in structures, payments and competition. But a revolution in values.

One that will provide excellent care to our patients. Where in every interaction we pinch ourselves at the honour we have been given to be privy to their secrets and pain—and as Don Berwick says, "being allowed to be guests in their lives."

My message to you is simple and clear. My son wanted to do medicine because of what he saw me and my friends do: care. If we want to keep serving the best interests of our patients, we must reject the language of the market and embrace the language of caring. And keep telling our stories.

Excerpt from "REJECT THE LANGUAGE OF THE MARKET AND EMBRACE THE LANGUAGE OF THE CARING"
Address by CLARE GERADA, Chair, Royal College of General Practitioners
Delivered at RCGP Annual Primary Care Conference, Liverpool, England, October 2011

How to Make Your Speech "Sticky" (& Why You Should)

Aim to give speeches that "stick"—that get and keep a listener's attention.

Why? Because if you don't, people *stop listening*.

You'll know this is happening when you see electronic gadgets pulled from briefcases, pockets, and purses.

When listeners lose interest, they start texting, checking their laptops for emails, surfing the Web. Mentally—and sometimes physically—they simply go away. Even good speakers aren't immune to some "electronic absence." But dull and boring speakers are guaranteed an absent audience.

Obviously, no speaker begins a speech or presentation with the intention of boring an audience. And, admittedly, audiences expect a lot today.

Keep this in mind: The attention span of the American adult is now six to seven minutes—the time between a batch of commercials.

There are several reasons for this, but that's the topic of a different book. What's important for speakers to know is that, today, 18 minutes is a long time for a speech. Fifteen minutes is closer to the recommended length. If you go longer than 15-18 minutes, you need to be absolutely wowing them. And wowing an audience requires considerable skill and preparation.

So, speeches today have to be more of everything—shorter, tighter, more poignant, more memorable, more sticky than ever before—because people's attention spans are shorter than ever.

You need to begin your speech or presentation with an attention grabber, make your points clearly and memorably, and then finish your presentation with a stirring, confident and *intentional* conclusion.

FORMULA FOR SPEAKING WELL:
Come in,
Make your point.
Make it clear.
Make it memorable.
Then get out.

In short, begin well, end well, and be compelling in the middle.

How to begin—

Bob Dole's

Most Memorable Speech

While he could look back on an impressive career in the U.S. Senate, Bob Dole was generally deemed an uninspiring speaker when he was a Presidential candidate. In *The Choice*, Bob Woodward's book on Bob Dole's 1996 campaign for the Presidency against incumbent President Bill Clinton, Woodward makes an important observation.

Woodward notes that a key speech for Dole would be his response to President Clinton's State of the Union Address. Dole dutifully rehearsed. But he was, as Woodward says, "stiff and ill at ease," as he presented his speech. "After several minutes," Woodward says, "he got better, but he was still shaky."

Dole and his advisers felt he had done well. But the next day, the media reviews for Dole's speech and for his style as a speaker were nearly uniformly critical with Republican Senator Jesse Helms declaring it the "worst performance" he'd ever seen.

As Woodward notes, even though Dole may have upped his game as a speaker in his speech that evening, he and his staff failed to realize that the Senator would not be judged against his own past performances—but against the speaking skills and public persona of Bill Clinton.

Contrasted against the youthful President Clinton—one of the nation's all-time most gifted orators—Dole faced a competitor who proved impossible for him to best.

And yet, observers have sometimes wondered if Senator Dole might have stood a better chance with coaching that could have helped him overcome his weakest areas as a speaker and public persona.

In speeches and other public appearances he gave following the 1996 election, he has shown a more engaging public persona and speaking style. This happened when he opened a speech not too long after his defeat by reaching out very sincerely to women in the audience and urging them to encourage their husbands and fathers to schedule checkups for prostate cancer (a form of cancer he had survived).

It was totally unexpected, but he was so passionate about having worked his way through prostrate cancer that he leapt off the stage and into the hearts of the audience by issuing this direct challenge on a very personal subject.

Who would start a just-the-facts business speech with this kind of message? But he did—and many people were wowed by the "new" Bob Dole.

Based on his history as a speaker, no one would have expected him to capture an audience and blow them away with opening remarks on a sensitive subject. But he did.

In short, he had it in him to connect powerfully with audiences—but he had not made coaching for public speaking a high enough priority when he was preparing for his 1996 Presidential run.

Would it have made a difference if he had? Anything is possible.

> One person with passion is better than forty people merely interested.
>
> — E. M. Forster

Vautier's Words to the Wise

Take the time to practice and thoroughly familiarize yourself with the first three lines of your speech. Always practice them out loud.

Should you memorize the lines? No, we don't recommend memorization. When you memorize, what happens if you forget a word or a phrase? If you're like most of us, you have to go back to the beginning and start again. Familiarization is different—it allows you to *own* the "rhythm" of the opening remarks.

Familiarizing himself with his opening lines is a technique Ronald Reagan adopted early in his career when he worked as a radio commentator. He discovered that by knowing the first three lines in a prepared script cold, the rest of his patter sounded "natural."

Here's why this is important: The opening lines of a speech are the most dangerous time for most presenters. Generally speakers are most nervous when they launch a speech or presentation. But what happens if you really *know* the first two or three slides, and the first two or three minutes of your presentation? Here's what will happen: You will ace the opening of your speech.

And if you ace the opening, you'll find you are then "in the zone." But stumble in those opening minutes, and you know you just muffed it. And everybody knows you just muffed it. And they know you know you muffed it. It's hard to recover from that. So, don't muff it! Practice, practice, practice your opening lines and the muffing problem is a non-issue.

7 – Delivery Options— Informal to Formal

- Looks Matter: Your Presentation Options—PowerPoint, Keynote & Prezi
- Speaking & Presenting Approaches: from Informal to Prepared Text
- Teleprompter & TelePresence Expand Your Effectiveness

Looks Matter:

Your Presentation Options—

PowerPoint, KeyNote & Prezi

At this writing, presenters who use slides have three primary options from which to choose: **PowerPoint, KeyNote and Prezi.**

- **PowerPoint**—this format has been around for some time and is familiar to most of us.

- **KeyNote**—this is the Mac version of PowerPoint. It is an excellent product. Many presenters feel the graphics in KeyNote are a "cut above." They can truly look spectacular.
- **Prezi**—this is the newest and most exciting option for creating visuals to accompany your speech or presentation. Originally Prezi visuals could be built only online. Now the company offers a desktop version of its program. Prezi allows you to create a series of images, words, graphs, and charts. Rather than a series of slides, you create an animated tour on a single "canvas." The tour follows a path you create that zooms in and out of the various elements you place on the canvas.

Death by PowerPoint?

We've all heard the phrase "death by PowerPoint." It refers to poorly prepared PowerPoint presentations—usually to presentations that overwhelm listeners/viewers with too much detail. Used properly, PowerPoint, and other presentation softwares, can add welcome visual components to a speech or presentation. Visuals can and should reinforce the verbal content of your speech or presentation.

Speaking & Presenting Approaches: from Informal to Prepared Text

As an executive (or someone on the executive track), you will experience a range of speaking options. You might on occasion be called upon to simply speak off the cuff (extemporaneously). This is the least formal of your delivery options. By definition, you have little chance to prepare for an extemporaneous, or impromptu, speech.

A little less informally, you may choose to give a talk from notes (i.e., not from a full text, but rather from bullet points).

Note: For informal speeches, we encourage speakers to use a tool called *Speak from Notes*[©]. *Speak from Notes* is a formatted speech organizer designed by Vautier Communications to help presenters sequence their thoughts effectively. It is made of heavy card stock that folds down the center. We believe it works better than the usual index cards for an informal presentation. If you would like this useful tool, e-mail us at John@VautierCommunications.com. We'll be pleased to send you a complimentary *Speak from Notes*.

Also in the informal delivery range: You can distribute a handout (printed material listing the gist of your messages). You can then walk your audience through key points or sections of your handout, elaborating on each point.

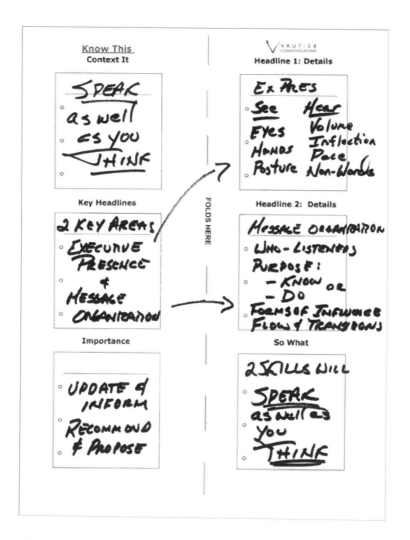

One side of the Vautier Communications *Speak from Notes*© (above) provides a one-page universal organizational tool for informal "Know This" speeches. The opposite side provides a universal organizational outline tailored to "Do This" speeches.

Speakers also may find themselves presenting in semi-formal situations. These include internal company videos, webinars, and media interviews. Each of these presentation situations requires a slightly different set of skills. Your speech coach or one of your company's communications professionals can assist you with the fine points of preparing for company videos and Webinars. See Chapter 8 for the how-to's of handling media interviews.

On the more formal end of the public speaking spectrum, you may opt to present using visuals created with presentation software such as those noted above.

Or you may present a speech using a prepared text—either written by yourself or by a speechwriter.

Speeches that the media or shareholders parse carefully for nuances of meaning, or speeches that deal with issues about which legal concerns exist, often are written to be presented verbatim. A prepared-text speech can be read from a text on a lectern, or from a teleprompter.

The art of speaking

from a prepared text

Prepared text speeches should not *appear* to be read.

There is an art to delivering a prepared text speech so that your delivery appears natural. There also is an art to writing such texts.

A speech text written by a good speechwriter sounds like natural dialogue when delivered by the speaker. The language will read well in print (which most natural dialogue fails to do). But it also will *sound* natural. With experience, some executives can deliver from a prepared text flawlessly, even without rehearsing first. This usually happens with speakers who are in great demand and are constantly at the podium.

For most executives it is advisable to hold "live" rehearsals of major speeches they plan to deliver from prepared texts—at least two rehearsals, and preferably three. The speechwriter and a speech coach, or a member of your organization's communications team—someone who is able to provide quality feedback—should be present as support.

On Simplicity:

"One should use common words to say uncommon things."

— Arthur Schopenhauer

"Simplicity is the ultimate sophistication."

— Leonardo da Vinci

Simplicity also works

Visual reinforcement of the points you make doesn't always need to be high tech. Karl Rove has made a "little white board" (a small dry-erase board) a hallmark of his speaking and presenting style. He often shows the audience, or holds up to a camera (depending on the situation), a simple graphic or a few key words on the white board.

A simple visual like this reinforces the verbal information he presents with additional visual information. It also is unique and memorable.

For the presenter, it has an added benefit: It forces the presenter to simplify key messages down to a few words, or a little graphic. This helps a presenter focus on the message with greater clarity.

Teleprompter

& TelePresence

Above: a teleprompter configuration popular with some speakers: two monitors are placed on the floor, and reflect the text of the speech up onto the Lucite panels on either side of the podium. The panels appear to be clear glass to the audience, but the speaker can read the text of his speech from them. A teleprompter operator advances the text to match the speaker's rate of speaking.

A speaker unfamiliar with the use of teleprompter technology should receive coaching in the use of this technology prior to using it for the first time to deliver a speech or a presentation.

TelePresence enables technology to save executives time and travel costs while duplicating the feel and benefit of face-to-face meetings.

Image courtesy of Fuelrefuel

The teleprompter sometimes sparks derisive comments from people. This always surprises us. People who deride teleprompters as "dishonest" or "artificial" don't take into account two aspects of public speaking:

1. That the importance of some occasions (not to mention legal concerns) sometimes requires the use of prepared remarks, read—sentence by sentence—by the speaker.

2. The options for delivering formal remarks like this are limited to, a) the executive reading from the text on a lectern in front of him, b) the executive using a teleprompter (reading from monitors reflecting onto glass panes positioned so that the executive appears to be speaking extemporaneously).

While highly experienced speakers—and those who take the necessary time to rehearse and prepare—can read from a printed speech text well, many speakers reading from a hard copy text are too obviously reading. For them, a teleprompter is an excellent option.

A teleprompter is an excellent option for the delivery of a formal speech, one that requires the speaker read from a speech text.

As a listener who would you rather listen to? A speaker delivering from a teleprompter with as close to natural delivery as is possible? Or a speaker who drops her head to read from a paper on a lectern and peeks up at you every now and then as she reads?

We've all changed phones as telephone technology advanced—from rotary phones to simple cell phones to smart phones. Why stick with an outmoded system for delivering a formal speech? At this writing, you can rent a teleprompter, complete with operator, for $350 for an afternoon. It's quick to set up and it works beautifully. Why not utilize this technology?

Certainly, have the entire speech script on the lectern in front of you as a backup. But use a teleprompter. It's the 21st century version of "speaking from a prepared script." TelePresence is another option for executives. Speeches can be delivered seated and the audience includes those physically in the meeting room with you, and those at another location you see via video camera, and vice versa.

The good news is, it's easy to master the use of both teleprompter and TelePresence. In actual fact, it should only take 20 minutes of training to familiarize anyone with how to deliver a speech with a teleprompter, or to use TelePresence.

But if an executive fails to take the time needed to familiarize himself with these aids, his performance with either may be less stellar than he would like it to be.

Savvy leaders take the time to master communications technologies.

Vautier's Words to the Wise

Writing a speech that is to be presented word for word as written is a special skill. It requires the ability to "write for the ear." If you are not confident you have mastered this skill, and you need to present a speech you will read verbatim, it is a good idea to engage the services of your communications team, or of a professional speechwriter to prepare the text, and of a public speaking coach to help you prepare to deliver the speech.

8 – From Sharing a Viewpoint to Dealing with the Unexpected

- Sharing a Viewpoint: The Art of the Short Message
- Q&A (Standard, Hostile, & Relentless)
- There Should Be No Surprises
- How to Respond Effectively Under Pressure
- Put the Shovel Down! (Mitt and Rick and the 3 Departments)

Interacting with

Your Listeners—How To's

One key skill executives need to master is the formula for sharing a viewpoint in under 30 seconds. Sharing a viewpoint is a "whole life skill." It's called that because you will use it frequently in your professional and personal life—most often in less formal settings.

I call sharing a viewpoint the art of the short message. And this is a very important skill to master.

You need to know how to deliver a "short message" those times when people don't want to hear a speech or a presentation, but just a quick summary of what you think about an issue or a topic. In other words, they want your viewpoint.

There are three, and sometimes four, elements to presenting your viewpoint effectively.

Here is the formula:
- Topic
- Viewpoint
- Evidence
- Tieback (optional)

Example: Presentation of Viewpoint

Topic
"Let me tell you what I think is going to happen with the World Series.

Viewpoint
"I think the San Francisco Giants are going to win. I think they're going to do it in six games."

Evidence
"And the reason I say that is, they've got great pitching, they've got great batters, and all of them are playing at the top of their game this year."

Tieback (optional)
"And that's why I think the Giants are going to win it in six games."

That's the formula in action.

To state a viewpoint, all you need are the first three components: topic, viewpoint, and evidence. If you choose to add, "And that's why I think . . ." that's the optional tieback.

With my clients, I suggest three lead-ins for the topic, viewpoint, and evidence elements, and for the optional tieback, as follows:

RECIPE FOR A VIEWPOINT

- *Topic lead-in:* "I want to say something about . . . "
- *Viewpoint lead-in:* "The way that I see it is . . . "
- *Evidence lead-in:* "And the reason I say that is . . ."
- *Tieback lead-in:* "And that's why I think . . . "

Those first three lead ins are key to structuring a viewpoint. All I have to do is finish those first three lead ins, and I've presented a complete viewpoint each and every time.

Most people find this "recipe," or format, for presenting a viewpoint useful. It enables them to advance their viewpoints effectively because it automatically organizes their thoughts.

When will you need to use the viewpoint format? In meetings and casual conversation—in various business settings, including both meetings, and casual conversation at the water cooler, and when socializing at business functions.

When an idea comes up and you have an opinion to offer on something, you'll find the viewpoint format handy. In fact, the most frequent messages we deliver are our viewpoints.

Example:
"Let me say something about the flights to Pittsburgh this weekend. I don't think you can depend on them. And the reason I say that is, the Weather Channel predicted a hailstorm. And last month, when we had a hailstorm, the flights to Pittsburgh were delayed, and I found I had to drive from Chicago to Pittsburgh to keep my appointments."

We're constantly sharing organized viewpoint "mini" messages—almost always in conversation. They're short—30 seconds or less. Why is this important in a business setting?

Because it is important for you to offer viewpoints on certain business occasions—to provide direction on a topic, or an initiative, or a vision. (You do this gently, of course.) Again, these are "mini" messages, short self-revelatory comments—not a full-blown speech or presentation.

In addition, before you sign a deal, or do business with potential colleagues, they will want to know several of your viewpoints before they commit to working with you. They also will expect you to be able to share your viewpoints logically and clearly. The mini-recipe ensures that you do so.

Sharing viewpoints effectively also is an element of building executive presence because you're showing your rational thinking power—you're not just stating, "Here's what I think. End of story." You're giving evidence. You're giving a mini speech.

When I coach, I always coach or teach the art of sharing a viewpoint before I coach or teach how to handle Q&A situations. That's because both utilize the same format.

The only difference is that viewpoint is usually driven by something I personally may want to talk about, while Q&A is driven by a question an interviewer wants me to answer. Once you're in a Q&A situation, when you answer a question, you do it the same way you present a viewpoint—except that you start with the viewpoint lead-in ("The way I see it is . . .") because, in Q&A, the questioner has already stated the topic ("Tell me something about . . .").

An executive dealing with a contentious matter needs to master the facts, and develop his organization's viewpoints—the messages he will deliver in regard to the contentious matter. He also needs to develop arguments that will support his messages. He needs to be consistent.

Q&A

How do you handle Q&A?

Simple. When asked a question, you answer the question directly. Then you *develop* the answer ("And the reason I say that is . . ."). As noted, it's the same process you use to present a viewpoint.

In stating a viewpoint, you affirm something. In answering a question, you respond to something. But you use the same formula for presenting information in both cases.

Consistency Is Key

Aim to deliver consistent viewpoints, and consistent answers.

If you change your viewpoints/answers, especially when dealing with controversial issues, the ground beneath you—understandably—gets shaky fast.

You need to be consistent. And everybody in your organization also needs to be consistent. You need to have three or four arguments you can present on any key issue. And all of the arguments need to fit into an overall consistent framework.

U.S. Presidents have turned to expert advisers like David Gergen, Karl Rove, and David Axelrod to help them shape their messages in key and/or controversial areas. That is how important they deem consistency in messaging.

Messages are agreed upon and Presidential advisers ensure that the arguments supporting the messages also are consistent. In corporations, executives can rely on their communications department's expertise to assist them in the same way.

Message versus Response

- A **message** is defined as "what you're going to say on a given subject." If you speak on a subject, always **put the message up front** (i.e., state the key facts up front—in your first few sentences—without a long preamble.)

- A **response** is defined as what you're going to say when you're asked about a given subject. If you answer a question, **answer the question directly.** ("Directly" means you give the questioner the information he requested without going off on a tangent before getting to the point.)

When you become known as an executive who **puts the message up front** and who **answers the question directly**, you will get a reputation for directness. People within your organization and outside of it will respect and appreciate that. Give questioners the answers they seek as soon as they ask. Don't make them wade through, and wander around in, "the what that's buried in the why."

Note: An executive on the way up needs to learn to work with his organization's communications team. A company's communicators can proactively help a leader to get his messaging right. Your communications team will ensure your messages are both suitable to various occasions and consistent.

Politics versus Business

Politicians don't always "answer the question directly." Politics has its own unique requirements.

Business is different. As a steward of organizational resources, you owe people accurate and direct information. In business, you have an audience that includes your shareholders and your board. They expect to be informed based on what you've made public with Wall Street. You need to drive results and deliver on expectations. As you do this, you need to keep a clear channel of communication along the way. In business, transparency is prized. Mislead the Street, and your credibility is gone. Sometimes the consequences are devastating. Think of some of the headlines we've seen in recent history. Exxon is a spectacular example.

In business, if you get caught in a lie, or a stretch of the truth—you hurt yourself, and you hurt your organization.

Business leaders can expect media interviews. Media interviews can be challenges or opportunities—or both. It is important to know how to prepare for the various kinds of interviews you will encounter.

Q&A

(Standard)

In a "standard" Q&A—i.e., with a friendly or neutral (not hostile) questioner—aim to answer each question as directly as possible. Provide the facts, as you know them, and then develop the answer. You can use one or more of your SPEAK options—see Chapter 6— to develop each answer.

When you answer a question directly and then develop the answer, you come across as credible, forthright, and transparent. When you "talk around" an answer, or beat around the bush, you impress listeners as evasive or untrustworthy—as "hiding something."

If there is some reason you can't answer a question directly, you are no longer in a standard Q&A format situation. You are, for whatever reason, on the defensive. See the next few sections for more on this.

Interacting

with Listeners:

the 3 Levels

A business or civic leader needs to be able to interact successfully with his audience in the Q&A session that generally follows a formal presentation. He also needs to interact in a polished fashion when he is interviewed by the media.

Related to these skills, there are three levels of interaction with listeners a leader needs to master.

Level 1—straightforward Q&A
In Level 1 exchanges, questioning is friendly, not hostile. Listeners/questioners simply want more information or a little further explanation.

Ninety-five percent of Q&A situations and media interviews are of the straightforward variety. In Level 1 exchanges, the speaker or interviewee listens to the questions asked, and then delivers the answers. You use the viewpoint formula provided earlier in this chapter for shaping a complete and well-rounded direct answer.

Level 2—hostile questioning

You will encounter a hostile Q&A once in a great while, and you need to be prepared.

Here is how you handle a hostile questioner: You master the art of the rephrasal.

In hostile Q&A situations, questions sometimes are formulated in a way that makes it impossible for you to answer the question as presented. In answering, stay true to the issue. Don't spin it. But re-word the question you've had lobbed at you.

An example: XYZ Chemical Company has spilled chemicals into a lake near its plant. A reporter thrusts a mike into the CEO's face as he leaves work for the day. The camera is rolling as the reporter asks: "Was it greed or ignorance that caused you to dump chemicals into the lake?"

If the CEO chooses one of the options the reporter offers in that question, he needs to admit he is "greedy" or "ignorant." The question is unanswerable, as asked.

To answer this kind of hostile question, the CEO first needs to rephrase it.

But he needs to stay true to the issue.

That means he needs to remove the emotional, accusatory overlay and find the nugget of fact the question contains—in this case, that nugget is: How did the chemicals get into the lake?

So, the CEO repeats the reporter's question, but rephrases it as: "How did the chemicals end up in the lake?"
The original, hostile question focuses on "why" (greed or ignorance). The rephrasal focuses on "how" (process failure).

If the CEO sticks with explaining the "why" the way the hostile questioner has presented it, he is placed on the defensive. If he shifts to explaining "how," he can explain a process that occurred. At the end of the process, chemicals ended up in the lake. Presented this way, neither "greed" nor "ignorance," but rather, a fault in the process, explains the spill.

The CEO then answers the question, as rephrased. In this case, the answer is that the spill occurred when the plant shut down for preventive maintenance. Again, at this point, the viewpoint logical format for providing a complete and well-rounded direct answer can be utilized.

In providing a well-rounded direct answer, the CEO *develops* the answer by presenting the facts in a clear and straightforward manner: "Let me take you through the time period from 9:30 pm when we shut down for preventive maintenance, to 11:30 pm, when the spill occurred. Here's what happened."

You can't always substitute "how" for "why." But in many cases, you can. When you do, it enables you to respond effectively while also defusing highly charged questions.

Level 3 is when you know ugly and brutal questions will be lobbed at you—and you prepare for them.

To rephrase a hostile question, think of the six journalistic questions meant to determine facts: who, what, when, where, why, and how?

Rephrase the hostile question so that it elicits facts, without the emotional overlay.

Level 3—relentless questioning

Condoleezza Rice provided an excellent example of how to handle Level 3 questioning when she was grilled by Richard Ben-Veniste at the 9/11 hearings.

Secretary Rice knew what was coming (that Ben-Veniste was going to hammer her with questions about the Presidential Daily Briefing, or PDB, President Bush was given shortly before 9/11—specifically about "what the President knew, " and "when he knew it.")

Knowing this, she pre-organized three responses (three things she was going to say) about the PDB, (plus two additional responses that she used less frequently).

Her three main points were:
- The PDB was a historical document.
- There was no new information in the document to pursue.
- There was nothing actionable in the document.

Her additional two points were:
> a) The FAA had been warned of possible hijackings, and
> b) The FBI and all of its field offices were investigating possible al-Qaeda cells across the U.S.—specifically in Brooklyn (New York), and Boston (Massachusetts).

So, she had five "places" she circled back to and used to respond to Ben-Veniste's persistent and relentless questioning. She stuck to her guns and left the meeting without losing any ground to her interrogator.

To handle Level 3 situations as well as this, you need to:
- *Know* what questions you are likely to be asked.
- *Prepare* your responses.
- *Be disciplined* in sticking to those responses.

What if you're approached and blindsided by a hostile questioner?

If you're approached and blindsided, you have two options.

Option 1:

You can say, "We will have a response, but we're not at a point where I'm prepared to respond to that right now." Or, "We will have a statement on that. It won't be released until later in the week, and I'm not prepared to give one now."

Option 2:

Be gracious and keep moving without responding. Because someone asks a question does not mean you need to answer. If a reporter and cameraman pursue you as you walk though the airport, or on your way to your ride home, be polite, be gracious, and keep moving.

When do you choose not to respond to the media?

With certain sensitive issues, to respond to questions would only "give the story legs" (keep it alive). Making a comment in these instances is like putting wood on the fire, and you may need to resist taking a position.

An example: A few years ago, when the auto industry was in peril, one high-level executive was "discovered" to be using a company jet to travel home on weekends.

What might, at first glance, have seemed an abuse of power, actually was a perk that had been negotiated into the executive's contract some time before the industry faced its crisis.

Nevertheless, one Detroit reporter dogged the executive, trying to get him to comment. The executive politely declined, eventually opted to give up the perk, and the story quietly went away without seriously denting the executive's or the company's image.

In the above example, given the climate of the times and the state of the auto industry, even though no wrongdoing had taken place, a discussion of executive compensation and perks would have fallen on unsympathetic ears. Neither the reporter, nor his reading audience would have viewed any explanations benignly.

How to Respond Effectively

under Pressure

If you are questioned under pressure (i.e., by a hostile, aggressive questioner)—whether in a media interview, or while providing testimony—you need to deliver a consistent viewpoint/answer/ response.

Blindsided? You shouldn't be

By the way, as an executive, if you're surprised by a reporter's or interviewer's hostile question or questions, you probably haven't been supported the way you need to be. If this happens more than once, you may be too insulated. Your staff may be hesitant to bring you bad news.

There should be

no surprises

Ask yourself: Are you making it difficult for your staff to communicate with you? If so, change that. You need to stay on top of developments on which you may be called to comment. Open lines to your communications experts should keep you informed and up to date.

If you *have* made it clear you want to be kept abreast of developments in sensitive areas, and you're still getting surprised by reporters' questions, somebody has dropped the ball.

The people you surround yourself with should be monitoring news and issues related to your areas of responsibility. They should be constantly keeping you abreast of what's going on "out there."

Can you be blindsided, even so? Sure, on occasion you can. That's just life. But 95% of the time, your team should be keeping you informed of "developing news" so that you face very few surprises.

The strongest executives, those who lead companies known to communicate well, have very close and strong relationships with their corporate communications departments. In those companies, the executive vice president of corporate communications has a "seat at the table." (He or she is typically part of the inner circle of the organization's Executive Team.) This is true for leading companies like Ford Motor Company, Molex, Bosch, Allstate and Whirlpool. These organizations stand as excellent examples of companies that practice a strong partnership between the corporate communications function and the C-Suite.

Put the Shovel Down!

(Mitt and Rick

& the 3 Departments)

One of the most painful moments viewers saw in the 2012 Republican Primary was the debate in which Texas Governor Rick Perry was unable to name one of the three government agencies he said he would eliminate if elected President. (It was the Department of Energy.)

Perry couldn't remember the name of the department. He struggled to recall it, and then other candidates, and even the moderator, tried to help him. The impression left on the audience was less than stellar.

The reason Perry appeared to lose the thread was probably that he failed to prepare adequately in real-life practice situations. Even so, the moment might have been survivable if he hadn't allowed himself, his fellow candidates, and the moderator, to further prolong it.

When you're speaking or presenting, and you realize you've "fallen into a rabbit hole," your best option is to end the rabbit hole moment as quickly and neatly as possible.

When Governor Perry drew a blank, he should have said, "I'll get back to you on that third department. The other thing I want to point out is ...." and gone on to a new point. Not a perfect solution, admittedly, but it would have been much better than what transpired.

If you draw a blank, in other words, don't end with a Big Fail. Pivot to a new thought. Don't spin your wheels in the ditch, digging it deeper for yourself. Use that new thought as traction. Get out of the ditch. Climb out and head somewhere else. Again, a pivot might be a little awkward. But for Rick Perry, a little awkward would have been a lot better than the Big Mess of Awkward that he allowed to develop. That was the end of Presidential aspirations for him. It was an unrecoverable moment.

So—if a fail is looming—you finish that thought and then you put the shovel down. You don't try and continue to talk your way through it—because you *won't* be talking your way through it. You will be digging yourself deeper.

Speaking under Pressure

Awkward incidents can happen at any time. With today's omnipresent technology, a foolish moment can take on a life of its own. In fact, this is no longer something that's a rarity.

Bumble an answer and it can be captured on a cell phone video camera. And BAM! You're leading the news that night. For all the wrong reasons. You didn't expect it. You just gave the wrong answer at the wrong time and it was captured on audio or video.
Don't make the mistake of thinking that you're going to be insulated from potential BAM! moments. You won't be.

That's why you need to continually practice the skill set of speaking under pressure.

What's the best way to practice? Work with members of your communications team, with a professional speaking coach, or with a friend. Practice the art of delivering the short message (viewpoint), and of handling Q&A.

Optimally, you should practice with your communications team members. That is because your communications team will know about any sensitive questions you might be asked. That means you can practice with "real world" issues and the team can coach you knowledgeably on messaging.

Put aside 30 minutes every week to practice. Make it a habit, a constant thing. Just as you work out at the health club to keep in shape physically, you need to practice your communication skills to keep in shape verbally.

Why practice your "speaking under pressure" executive communications skills? To stay sharp. Because when you bumble a "rabbit hole" moment, *it is unfixable*.

Your communications team should constantly challenge and prepare you—both for what is going to happen and for what *might* happen. Your corporate communications team is there to ensure that the leaders of your organization represent the company well in the media. They are your front line.

9 - Communicating

to the C-Suite

- More vs. Better
- With the C-Suite, Put the Message Up Front
- Executive Summary How To's
- PowerPoint & the Difference between the Appendix and the Appendix

"Be sincere, be brief, be seated."

— Franklin D. Roosevelt

As an executive ascends the career ladder, his responsibilities and his compensation rise accordingly. Out of necessity, young executives quickly learn to manage time wisely. Up-and-coming executives also learn to minimize "face time" with the CEO and top officers of the company.

It seems counter-intuitive. Wouldn't an executive seeking to climb the ladder want as much face time with top leaders as possible? No, no, and no again.

C-Suite executives have tightly managed schedules, and time slots in which they need to accomplish specific tasks, and make decisions.

When you give a speech or make a presentation to a C-Suite executive, you demonstrate your understanding of how top management functions when you are brief and to the point and when you present key information that way also.

At church recently, our pastor dedicated his sermon to an appeal for contributions to the church's capital campaign. He got enthused, digressed, and spoke ten minutes longer than usual. As my wife and I were leaving the narthex, he asked, "How did I do?" I gave him a one-word critique. "Long."

My wife was mortified. She felt I had been too blunt. But I knew the pastor wanted honest feedback and I said, "Kit, so many people who speak confuse 'more' with 'better.' But 'more' is just 'more.'"

—John M. Vautier

More vs. Better

Most people agree that more is not necessarily better when it comes to Sunday sermons. The same certainly holds true for communicating with the C-Suite.

Very often "more" takes the speaker away from the central theme. Sometimes speakers end up lost in the woods that way. You can tell when a speaker has strayed from the "map"—what he'd planned to say. He begins to drop the non-words, the "ums" and "uhs."

When you communicate with senior executives: Know your message. Deliver the message. Period. Don't think, because you may be enjoying presenting, that the audience will enjoy listening longer than they expect to listen, or need to listen. In short: If you have advanced in your career to the point where you are communicating to the C-Suite, you need to make sure you know how to deliver speeches and presentations to their expectations.

Why brevity is necessary with the C-Suite

- Time is a most valuable commodity to executives. The higher up the chain of command they are, the more important the time executives have at their disposal becomes. Don't cause them to waste their time. Ensure that the time they spend with you is brief but *packed with value*.

- Putting the message up front also is important because today we all (C-Suite included) have shorter attention spans.

- Putting the message up front makes your input clear to your audience from the start—whether you are delivering a message, a viewpoint, a position, a response to a question, or an executive summary on a proposal/presentation. This helps them make decisions faster and better—and making decisions is what they are paid to do. Help them to do their jobs better and you will be appreciated.

With the C-Suite,

Put the Message Up Front

"Put the message up front" means provide your C-Suite audience with an Executive Summary version of your speech or presentation. An Executive Summary condenses your message to its essence. It should be short enough to fit on one or two sheets of paper. It should be three to four minutes long, tops. When you make a speech or presentation to C-Suite executives, be *prepared* to deliver all the facts and figures and details they might possibly ask about. But don't deliver all those details unless you are asked to do so. Deliver *only* the Executive Summary.

If they want to hear more, they will ask.

In a typical Executive Summary, you present your information in the form of short answers to the following questions on any given issue or concern:

- **What?**
- **Why?**
- **Timing?**
- **Cost?**

When you finish, give your listeners a choice as to whether they want to hear more.

Executive Summary

How To's

'We don't have any water'

After the nuclear disaster that occurred in Fukushima, Japan, in 2011, the Board of Directors at a large U.S. energy company responsible for a nuclear power plant summoned the plant manager to a meeting.

They told him they wanted him to bring data that would reassure them that a Fukushima-type incident would not occur at the facility for which they were responsible.

The plant manager went to the meeting and told them simply: "You don't need to worry about a Fukushima-type incident here *because we don't have any water.*"

He went on to explain that everything at Fukushima had worked well. When the earthquake hit Japan, the Fukushima generator shut down, but backup generators kicked into action, as intended, and started the cooling process. What created the catastrophe at Fukushima *was the tsunami that followed the earthquake.* The tsunami took out the backup generators. As the U.S. plant manager explained, "If we have an earthquake here— which we haven't had for 100 years, by the way—the reactors will cycle down, but we have backup generators—and we won't have a tsunami come in and take our backup generators out."

This very short presentation was exactly what the executive team wanted to hear—the expert's analysis and conclusion on a crucial issue. And that was all they needed to hear.

TIP: It is optimal to schedule a presentation to the C-Suite for early in the morning or early in the afternoon. Why? If you are scheduled late in the morning or late in the afternoon, the preceding speakers may use up more than their scheduled time. So, if you were scheduled to speak at 11 am, but aren't ushered in until 11:20, you'll be forced to adjust your content and the length of your talk to the revised timing. It you're scheduled for 8 am, you are more likely to kick-off at 8 am.

PowerPoint &

The Difference Between

The Appendix

& the Appendix

PowerPoint. Where do we begin?

PowerPoint seems to exasperate all of us. Every client we have worked with has a love/hate relationship with PowerPoint. The most common complaint I hear is, "What can we do about improving PowerPoint? There are just too many details in PowerPoint presentations."

The grievances about PowerPoint are pretty much on target.

Good slides should be 1) simple, 2) feature visuals that reinforce the messages of your arguments, 3) feature only a few words or statistics.

But it is very common to see PowerPoint slides with no visuals, or with complex graphics, or featuring lots of text in a font difficult for viewers to read.

Judging from the PowerPoints many of us are subjected to, the temptation for PowerPoint presenters is to do a data dump on viewers. But this is a mistake. Messages get obscured. Audiences lose focus.

Keep your presentation simple.

But what if the audience actually does want to know how many gizmos versus grommets we sold in the fourth quarter five years ago versus last year?

There's a simple solution. Create your data dump slides, complete with gizmo and grommet information—and plunk them into the appendix. All the information that you prepare—just in case they ask—should be in the appendix.

The appendix will give you the security of knowing you have the information handy if you need it.

But, up front, in the simple and easily absorbed slides you prepare, present your key messages. The slides you actually show should reinforce your arguments with a series of simple visuals, or with only a few words or a simple graph on each slide.

> Store *all* the data you *may* need in your appendix. But
>
> don't present all that information—the details—unless
>
> it is requested. If you present *all the information*,
>
> peoples' eyes will glaze over. It will be too much.

Oh, the difference between the appendix and the appendix? One is a worthless organ that many people have taken out. The other appendix (the one in your PowerPoint presentation) is also worthless—in the sense it will drain energy from your presentation if you present all the information it contains. But, of course, you won't do that. Your PowerPoint appendix will serve as your parking spot for the grimble you hold in reserve unless it's asked for.

Grimble—a colloquialism used to describe the too-detailed information a good speaker should avoid presenting in a speech or presentation.

A Lesson from The C-Suite

Early in my career, I coached the CFO for General Motors Asia Pacific. This was before slides were digitalized into PowerPoints. As I usually do with clients, I asked him to send me a copy of his presentation before I joined him for a coaching session.

He said, "I can't—it's 120 slides." I was taken aback. How on earth, I asked him, could he present 120 slides? "Oh, no," he said. "I'm only going to present 20. The other 100 are the appendix. That's in case they ask me questions." He had it right. That's the way to present to the C-Suite.

How do you locate that particular bit of information in your appendix?

Create an "index" to your slides—a sheet of paper containing the number of each PowerPoint slide in the appendix. (Click on "View" and then on "Slide Sorter" in the PowerPoint menu to see the number of each slide.) On the paper index, next to each number, jot down a brief description of what the slide contains alongside the number. *Note:* In PowerPoint "SlideShow" mode, you can summon up a particular PowerPoint slide by number—e.g., if you keystroke 56, PowerPoint will take you to slide 56.

10 - What You Do Speaks More Loudly Than What You Say

- Doing the Right Thing: Bill Ford & the Rouge Disaster
- Likability—Work on It
- Listen & Silent Have the Same Letters

Doing the Right Thing: Bill Ford & the Rouge Disaster

On February 1, 1999, a gas explosion killed six employees and injured 24 more at Ford's Rouge Plant in Dearborn, Michigan. The Rouge was the first plant Henry Ford, the company's founder, built. In some ways, it represents the heart of the company.

When the disaster occurred, Bill Ford—Henry Ford's great-grandson—was CEO of Ford. As soon as he heard what had happened, he made preparations to head over to the plant.

His communications advisers voiced concerns about his decision. They advised he issue a statement rather than visit in person. Their concerns were genuine. The site would be full of reporters and cameramen recording the aftermath of a fiery explosion—a ruined building and badly injured people. It was the opposite of the upbeat media events in which communications team memberss typically seek to position their CEOs.

"You can't go over there," one of them cautioned him.

Bill Ford answered, "I can't not go over there. They're family."

When he arrived, his eyes filled with tears. People wept with him. The story has become part of Ford Motor Company's history and culture. It is part of what makes Ford unique and appealing—the family ownership of the company and the sense of extended family among many Ford employees. Bill Ford had no thought of building Ford's brand or adding to the company's blue sky value when he headed to the Rouge Plant that awful day. He did what his instinct told him was right.

Traditional thinking would be, "I'll let corporate communications manage it." Probably any other executive would have deferred to the recommendations of his corporate communications team. And Bill Ford opted not to. At his core, he felt it was the right thing to be at the site of the heart-wrenching event. He felt the right thing to do was to physically be there. His actions demonstrated his care and concern and exemplify real leadership communication at its best.

Likability—

Work on It

Never underestimate the power of likability. The day of the cold and distant CEO is over. Bill Clinton is an example of the power of likability. President Clinton was brought before Congress and almost impeached. But many of his admirers wished he could have run for a third term. At this writing, his popularity is at an all-time high. The reason is, in large part, his likability.

Between us, we have coached two people who have met Bill Clinton and their experiences with the former President illustrate why he is so well regarded by so many.

Here are the experiences of those two people—we'll call them "Joe" and "Alice."
At a conference where Bill Clinton got up to go to the restroom, Joe—an admirer—followed him, hoping for a chance to exchange a few words. Joe was held back by security, but when Bill Clinton emerged from the restroom, he noticed Joe standing with the Secret Service men. The former President approached Joe, and said, "Hey, sorry about that. That's just what goes on around here." He then shook Joe's hand. How can the recipient of that thoughtful attention help but become an even greater fan for life?

Another encounter took place in midtown Manhattan. Another admirer, Alice, spotted Bill Clinton walking across the street. "So I made a beeline to him to introduce myself," Alice says. As with the other incident, security surrounded Alice. Again Clinton approached the new admirer and shook her hand. Another fan reinforced.

The point is: That likable public figure we see on the TV or hear on the radio, probably isn't too much different from the guy you would meet if you approached him on the street or at a conference center. Charismatic leaders project genuine likability because they have a mindset of genuinely liking their constituents—or they take the trouble to behave congruent with that mindset in their private as well as public actions. The impression each of us gets is: "He likes me back!" It's a consistent picture. (And it's only natural for us to strengthen our bonds with those who "like us back." That is how elections are won.)

Eliminate off-putting behavior/mannerisms

No woman has walked the earth more prepared to be President than Hillary Clinton. But when she ran against Barack Obama in the 2008 Democratic Primary, she couldn't get enough votes to win. She was not as able to project likability as her spouse.

In my opinion, what helped sink Hillary Clinton during that primary race was an off-putting manner in which she inflected her voice during some of her speeches. Somewhere she had picked up the mannerism of inflecting *every word* in some sentences. It sounded as if she were talking down to her audiences.

It's important to send that crucial "I like you" message when you're talking to people. She failed to do this. For all of us, it's a good idea to regularly "do an inventory" of ourselves to assess if we need to work at habits or mannerisms that may be off-putting to others. If needed, we can get feedback from friends and associates, or from a professional coach.

Listen & silent

Have the Same Letters

Denny McGurer, one of the world's leading executive coaches and a longtime associate of renowned leadership expert Ken Blanchard, tells the story of an executive whose firm had to deal with the aftermath of a disaster. We'll call the executive Sam. The disaster had impacted thousands of the company's customers. Denny had coached Sam who led his team in very successfully coping with an overwhelming workload under highly stressful conditions.

One of the executive's colleagues commented to Denny on how well the crisis had been handled saying, "I don't know what you've been feeding Sam, but could you send some along for the rest of us." "It's no mystery," Denny said. "Here's what Sam has been doing—he's been *listening.*"

Listening is very important. You learn a tremendous amount of information when you just listen.

But you can't listen when you're talking.

And you *need* to listen. Excuse my bluntness, but sometimes you need to *shut up* and listen.

Don't jump in too quickly. If you do, you can jump in before you've heard the whole thought someone else is expressing. You've got a piece of it and you think, "I'm gonna jump on this," and you do and you've got it wrong. If you'd waited just a few seconds longer, an extra (and critically important) bit of information would have been shared.

Listen.

On silence

Silence, by the way, is essential for listening.

Never underestimate the power of silence.

Sometimes, when the other guy is talking, and you feel you can't get a word in edgewise, *let him talk*. People who talk nonstop often talk themselves into a hole, or down a blind alley. Again, don't jump in too quickly.

> *"Silence cannot be misquoted."*
>
> —*Folk saying*

11 - In Conclusion

What we learned from the eighth graders at Thomas Middle School in Arlington Heights, Illinois

Every year, at the school the children in our family attend, 300 eighth graders get an assignment. They are told that, at Christmas break, they need to write a graduation speech to be delivered in June. It can be up to five minutes—no longer.

Then, from Christmas vacation until spring break, the students edit their speeches. When they return from spring break in early April, they compete in a "speech off." The "speech off" is a process for selecting the five best speeches. When only ten speakers remain in the running, the mayor and local business leaders get involved in judging to select the finalists.

The five best speakers speak at the graduation ceremony.

On graduation day, 3,000 people—friends and family—are seated in the auditorium to hear the speeches. At a recent graduation, one of the top speakers—a 14-year-old—delivered a remake of the pop tune, "Bye Bye, Miss American Pie." He called his speech, "Bye Bye, Gonna Be a High School Guy." He delivered the speech so well that all 3,000 people in the audience got to their feet and cheered.

As we tell our clients, if a 14-year-old's teacher can get him to do that, we know we can get them to master executive communications!

Performance coaching—it's like voting in Chicago

One very important aspect of executive communication I want to touch on here is performance coaching. Giving performance feedback to an associate or employee is called performance coaching.

Coaching means you provide feedback that's both positive and developmental. You encourage positive behaviors. (And you do so with a light touch.) You also nudge at the things that you don't want happening. (This too doesn't need to be harsh.)

> # You metaphorically swing your arm—and decide how high (or low) your palm lands.

But some people don't know how to do it. They see someone who reports to them act erroneously but can't bring themselves to comment. They avoid the performance coaching they need to do—at least they do until they hit a boiling point. Then they blast an underperforming or poorly performing employee. And the employee on the receiving end—not too surprisingly—thinks, "Gosh, where is this coming from?"

There's an old joke in Chicago. It dates back to the days of corrupt ward bosses who supposedly were given a case of liquor and a stack of $5 bills. The liquor and bills were distributed to generate votes for a given candidate. Since voters were rewarded in this fashion, some apparently voted more than once. So, the joke is that, in Chicago, you vote early—and you vote often.

That may not be an ideal way to get out the vote. But early and often *is* ideal for performance coaching.

You should be constantly delivering a metaphorical pat on the back—or a slap on the seat—to the folks you are responsible for training and developing. That's how you drive the behavior you want to see. It needs to be an ongoing, constant thing.

> *A word fitly spoken is like apples of gold in a setting of silver.*
>
> *—Proverbs 25:11*

An Invitation

To Speak As Well

As You Think

It is not uncommon for seasoned business executives to feel confident in their fields of expertise, yet find themselves struggling when it comes to expressing their ideas clearly and effectively to sales teams, clients and employees. And yet the ability to present well in front of a group is an essential skill for success at leadership levels in the business world.

Vautier Communications has successfully coached executives across the world to unleash the leader within—to "speak as well as they think." The results? Audiences are actively engaged, motivated, and inspired. The speaker and the message are elevated to new levels of status. Learn to present well at the podium and you earn respect and grow your opportunities. What happens next? The sky's the limit!

Vautier Communications team of experienced coaches look forward to helping you take your presentation skills to the next level. Contact us at 847-749-1930, or at john@vautiercommunications.com.

ABOUT THE AUTHORS

JOHN M. VAUTIER has, throughout his career, coached more than 1,000 CEOs and senior leaders, and more than 3,000 executives, sales professionals and next-generation leaders, developing and enhancing their leadership communication skills. He founded Vautier Communications in 2004 following a highly successful career as Vice President of Sales with Communispond, the company that established the executive communications industry, and where John sold, coached, and managed the sales force, and played an integral role in the company's success. John lives with his wife in Arlington Heights, Illinois.

JOHN J. VAUTIER graduated as a Sales Scholar from Illinois State University, and was recruited as a Sales Development Representative into Whirlpool's highly selective 'Real Whirled' Sales Talent Management Program. From there he was assigned a territory in Fort Worth, Texas, and managed key relationships on the National Account Team. After almost two years with Whirlpool, John returned to Chicago and joined Vautier Communications as an Account Executive and Coach. He's developed a number of key accounts and consistently earns high marks as an outstanding coach. He has a passion for physical fitness and aims to balance his professional goals with a healthy lifestyle.

17030164R00096

Made in the USA
Charleston, SC
23 January 2013